Fear Memory Integration

This book is dedicated to Jeffrey Duval, who taught me how to listen and to Howard Cameron, who taught me how to feel.

It is also dedicated to Marie and James, my paternal grandparents; Nick and Rosemary, my parents; Susan, my wife; David and Amelia, my children; and Tylor and Shayla, my beautiful grandchildren.

Fear Memory Integration

◆

A Natural Health Alternative to Conventional Psychotherapies

Jim Pullaro, PhD

iUniverse, Inc.
New York Lincoln Shanghai

Fear Memory Integration
A Natural Health Alternative to Conventional Psychotherapies

iUniverse books may be ordered through booksellers or by contacting:

iUniverse
2021 Pine Lake Road, Suite 100
Lincoln, NE 68512
www.iuniverse.com
1-800-Authors (1-800-288-4677)

ISBN-13: 978-0-595-36514-2 (pbk)
ISBN-13: 978-0-595-80948-6 (ebk)
ISBN-10: 0-595-36514-0 (pbk)
ISBN-10: 0-595-80948-0 (ebk)

Printed in the United States of America

Contents

CHAPTER 1   Introduction 1

CHAPTER 2   Literature Review. 7

- *The Imprint* 7
- *Memory*. 8
- *Memory Storage*. 9
- *Memory Retrieval*. 14
- *Memory and Stress* 21
- *The Continuum of PTSD*. 22
- *Primal Memories Generate Psycho-neurological Imbalances* 24
- *Human Development and the Roots of Neurosis*. 25
- *The Toxic Mind Hypothesis* 30
- *Arthur Janov's Evidence* 33
- *The Mind's Eye* 35
- *Homeopathy The Nature of Symptoms* 36

CHAPTER 3   Implications. 43

- *A Naturopathic Anatomy of Neurosis* 43
- *The Naturopathic Facilitation of Emotional Wellness General Considerations*. . . . 46
- *Provoking the Healing Crisis*. 51
- *Abreaction vs. Primalling*. 57
- *Some Parameters for the Facilitation of Emotional Wellness* 58
- *Other Environmental Considerations in Neurosis*. 60

CHAPTER 4   Conclusion 65

- *Primal Facilitation Is a Naturopathic Modality*. 65
- *Summary*. 69

- *Healing and Curing* *71*

APPENDIX   The Author's Doctoral Practicum Results 75

Sources Consulted 77
  Books
  Articles

Glossary of Terms 83

About the Author 87

1

Introduction

The intent of this work was to conduct theoretical research into the nature of neurosis: specifically, its cause and how the cause can be effectively addressed naturopathically. Previous to this undertaking, I had participated in the primal therapy process at Arthur Janov's Primal Center over a period of three years. During this time I found my emotional life improving noticeably, without the aid of psychotropic medication or behavioral modification programs. I was curious to know why these welcome changes could occur. This book is my attempt to understand why this naturopathic therapy is so effective.

The Diagnostic and Statistical Manual of Mental Disorders (DMS-IV), as of 2005, lists more than 340 separate mental disorders, which is 120 more than its predecessor, DSM-III-R.

Emotional disorders comprise a large portion of the most common psychiatric disorders. And many of these are related to the brain's fear system.

According to the Public Health Service, about 50% of mental problems reported in the United States (other than those related to substance abuse) are accounted for by anxiety disorders, including phobias, panic attacks, post-traumatic stress disorder, obsessive compulsive disorder, and generalized anxiety.[1]

Modern psychiatry has followed the lead of the medical profession in its search for disease processes as a cause of "mental illness." Currently psychiatrists are considering an underdeveloped orbitofrontal lobe of the brain as a possible example of neurotic pathology.[2] And altered levels of various neural transmitters are also being correlated with different conditions, such as depression. It is assumed that genetics is conditioning this alteration.

Poor parenting can lead to severe pruning of orbitofrontal neurons during the critical growth period. And some have argued that the resultant smaller-than-normal lobe may be a pathological process leading to neurosis in later life. One of the functions of this area of the brain is impulse control. Lower impulse control translates into abnormal behavior. But we must ask the question: what impulses are being under-controlled?

Low levels of different brain neurotransmitters, such as serotonin, are associated with conditions such as major depression. But, when we ask why these chemicals are low, faulty genetics is the assumed answer. Again, we assume a pathology exists that prevents the natural manufacture of serotonin in susceptible people; however, to date, there is no evidence of such a pathology.

Serotonin is a painkiller. The human body produces it and fifty other such powerful painkillers naturally.[3] Every second of our lives, our body successfully regulates millions of chemical reactions. Why would it be inept with its production of serotonin? Since it is a painkiller, a more logical explanation of serotonin depletion in some people might be that those people are using up their normal supplies in a process of excessive pain management. What is the source of this pain? It is clear that both arguments fail to address causal processes.

Because researchers have not been able to produce definite pathology, the mental health field has adopted an atheoretical treatment approach. That is, they make no assumptions about the cause of a particular disease. Indeed, the DSM-IV now defines a mental disorder as a "clinically important *collection of symptoms* that causes an individual distress, disability, or the increased risk of suffering pain, disability, death, or the loss of freedom."[4] This allows the profession to assume pathology exists and to treat individuals accordingly, without actually having to prove it. It is very clear by its definition of mental disorder that conventional psychotherapy has contented itself with the treatment of symptoms. In this "allopathic" model, therapists are treating symptoms (behaviors) as the disease itself, and behavioral and chemical treatments are designed to oppose or suppress those symptoms.

While these treatments can alleviate symptoms, they can never be curative. Everyone understands that cutting the leaves off of a weed does not prevent the leaves from growing back. One must remove the roots. In fact, pruning the leaves actually encourages the weed to produce a hardier growth of leaves. Within the domain of psychological treatment, this is reflected in the fact that chemical treatment must be periodically changed or increased to achieve the same result. And, in the case of behavioral treatment, support groups must be a lifelong endeavor. Or the individual substitutes alternate forms of dysfunctional behavior for the original ones. The human psyche is embedded in natural processes. Although treating the symptoms may appear to solve the problem as the symptoms abate, the underlying process, which generated the symptoms in the first place, continues to exist. Treatment of symptoms only tends to encourage chronic conditions. Neurosis is a chronic condition.

The naturopathic community defines illness as an imbalance in the harmony of cellular processes, brought on by an underlying condition of toxicosis. They argue that the newborn child carries just about every dangerous microorganism that exists. If the germ theory of illness is correct, why is it that most children do not succumb to the effects of virulent diseases? Human beings have been born into this "dangerous" environment for hundreds of thousands of years, yet disease is a relatively isolated event. Why is it that we are not all sick all of the time? Naturopaths have always believed that if the human body is getting what it needs to maintain its healthy functioning, then that functioning, fine-tuned over millions of years of evolution, will not allow the effects of dangerous substances to accumulate in the body, to the extent needed to support disease. *It is the combination of inadequate nutrition and inadequate cellular detoxification that creates the environment of disease.*

For over three hundred years, humans have known of the cellular basis of life. No one questions the veracity of this knowledge. Yet, for some reason, it does not inform the practice of psychotherapy.

Each and every living entity emerges out of the energy structure of its environment as a single cell, which rapidly divides into trillions of cells, all of which are literally afloat in a sea of nutrient-rich water. A vast ocean exists around each and every one of these cells all working together in harmony. The harmonious association of cells *is* the individual. The beating heart drives the ocean that is constantly flowing onto the membranes of these trillions of cells. A constant flow of arterial nutrients are moved through the membranes, and each cell accepts them to be used in its cellular processes. As the cells utilize the nutrients, they generate toxic byproducts. These byproducts are moved back toward the exterior of the cells and out onto the membranes to be swept away by venous currents. These currents flow onto the membranes of our organs of detoxification, move through these membranes, and move out into the environment. The detoxification processes are so critical to the smooth functioning of cellular processes that our bodies use an estimated 80 percent of our daily energy production to accomplish this task.[5]

On the cellular level, then, the individual is dependent upon the environment into which it emerges for all of the things that it needs for the proper unfolding of its genetic structure. And, *the nature of that environment conditions the nature of the expression of that genetic code.* The individual develops, inheriting the phenomenological or felt sense of "being healthy" as a consequence of the smooth running of this synergistic relationship. In naturopathic thought, "health" and "the smooth integration of object and environment" are synonymous concepts.

It is clear, then, that the cell and its environment—the individual and its environment—are interacting aspects of a single, indivisible process. The ancient Chinese concept of yin and yang most accurately conceptualizes this relationship.

If its environment is fully one-half of the individual's makeup, why do so many people resist examining the quality of the environment as a possible source of the generation of disease states?

Medical science has been dominated for over seventy years by the theory that people get sick because they are the victims of disease entities. Baker suggests that "people get sick because of a disruption of the dynamic balance that exists between themselves and their environment."[6]

Thirty-five years ago psychologist Arthur Janov developed a naturopathic psychological theory, which postulated an underlying, environmental cause for neurosis. He claimed to offer not a treatment of symptoms but a cure for neurosis. Recently some research, without referring to his work, has appeared to both mirror and substantiate his theories. It is time to reexamine a naturopathic model of neurosis, which offers the hope of healing, rather than just a lifelong management of chronic behavioral symptoms.

Janov's work is called primal therapy. Dr. Janov has been conducting his therapy for over thirty-five years and has generated a large body of data, which seems to substantiate, in concrete and scientifically demonstrable ways, the efficacy of his treatment program. Unlike his peers in the psychological community, Janov has postulated an etiology for neurosis, and his treatment purports to address its cause, rather than its symptoms. Janov's concept of neurosis presumes the operation of concrete *neurobiological processes.* Since the current psychological community has demanded that the study of mental illness be based upon observable phenomena and scientifically valid data, his ideas deserve close scrutiny by that community. This has not happened.

I hope that this book serves to stimulate a closer look at Janov's data. In this book, I have used the term "neurosis" to mean *all functional emotional disorders having no apparent histological cause.* This definition rules out all organic disorders, but includes those disorders that are presently associated with a presumed chemical imbalance of the brain. This category is critical because of Janov's unique theories of the etiology of such chemical imbalances (i.e., his belief that chemical imbalances are also symptoms). I have presented evidence that I found in current research in the areas of fear memory formation and retrieval and post-traumatic stress disorder, which supports Dr. Janov's theories.

Janov's theories postulate the existence of very unique and primitive body memories; therefore, to help clarify this concept, I have introduced a general theory of memory.

In order to understand Janov's concepts, one needs to have a basic understanding of how important the quality of the developing child's environment is to his psychosocial development. This requires a deep ecological understanding of human development. I have provided an example of such a theory of development.

I also present a theory that describes a possible neurological basis for Janov's theories. This theory postulates that chronic fear memory retrieval and repression cause a process of endogenous toxification of the nervous system. That is, the individual, through its environmentally conditioned behavior, actively participates in the toxification of its own nervous system.

Once one understands that chronic fear memory retrieval and repression and their subsequent neural toxification are the causes of neurosis, one might ask: how can this process be reversed? In answer to this question, I have offered a hypothesis for a naturopathic etiology of neurosis, along with some basic guidelines for the naturopathic reversal of the neurotic process.

After considering primal therapy within the operational framework of naturopathic thought, I present a discussion of its basic requirements as a naturopathic therapy.

During the course of my studies, I used my doctoral practicum to conduct a twelve-week longitudinal study of three men who volunteered to participate in a program of primal facilitation. The purpose of the study was to test Janov's claim that objectively verifiable and normalizing changes are effected by the process of primal therapy. The results of my study are located in the Appendix.

Chapter 1
Endnotes

1. LeDoux, J. (2002, August). <u>LeDoux Laboratory</u>.
   Available: <u>http://www.cns.nyu.edu/home/ledoux/overview.htm</u>

2. A.L. Schore, *Affect Dysregulation and Disorders of the Self* (New York: W.W. Norton & Company, Inc., 2003), 35.

3. A. Janov, *Why You Get Sick, How You Get Well: The Healing Power of Feelings* (West Hollywood, CA: Dove Books, 1996), 49.

4. J. Morrison, *DSM-IV Made Easy, The Clinician's Guide to Diagnosis* (New York: The Guilford Press, 2001), 8-9.

5. S. M. Baker, *Detoxification and Healing: The Key to Optimal Health* (New Canaan, CT: Keats Publishing, Inc., 1997), 141.

6. Baker, *Detoxification and Healing,* 173.

2

Literature Review

THE IMPRINT

Arthur Janov, PhD, trained in the Freudian tradition of psychotherapy. The Freudians believed that early childhood trauma somehow created neurosis in later life. In his early years, Freud believed that his patients' reports of childhood abuse were descriptions of fact. But, for various reasons, he later came to feel that the reports were a result of the tendency of children to fantasize. He then created intellectual constructs that could help to explain why children would fantasize about childhood abuse. His concepts of the Oedipus and Electra complexes were two such intellectual constructs. This decision on Freud's part relegated neurotic behavior to a realm of invisible psychic forces that eventually led to the mental health community's rejection of his definition of neurosis in the 1980's. As early as the publication of the DSM III, the editors had made the decision to drop the use of the term "neurosis." At that time psychiatrists were making a conscious effort to base diagnoses "on observable phenomena (e.g. behavior) and scientifically valid data."[1] Since neurosis, as the Freudians used the term, presumed the operation of invisible psychic processes, it did not fit the current model.

Like the younger Freud, Janov believed that his clients' reports of childhood trauma were real. But, if they were real, how could this early trauma continue to affect the person as an adult? How could the effects of the child's negative experiences endure throughout the years? Unlike Freud, who developed intellectual constructs as an explanation, Janov began looking for scientifically verifiable processes. What was the neurobiological mechanism of neurosis?

Janov theorized the existence of a "special category of memory" which he called imprints.

> Imprints, as I use the term, are repressed memories, which find their way into the biological system and produce distorted functions. These distortions can be both organic and psychological. The formation of

imprints takes place during early childhood development and falls off critically after about the age of ten.[2]

Once established, he says, these special body memories continually interfere with the individual's present-day behavior throughout life. They intrude into daily activities. One continually reacts to these intrusive, imprinted memories, rather than reacting directly to events in the present. In this way, behavior in the present appears distorted. As Janov states, (in the neurotic act-out) the feeling the individual is reacting to is correct, but the context of the feeling is wrong.

It is Janov's belief that the child can start recording these "body memories" as early as twenty-six weeks after conception, when the electrical activity of the cerebral cortex is well developed.[3]

MEMORY

Memory is nature's way of allowing us to project our experiences forward in time. Henderson has speculated that the human nervous system has two very distinct ways of doing this.[4] During the time that we are in our mother's womb, and for the first six years of life, a very primitive memory system is functional. This memory system encodes experience in terms of pleasant and painful sensorimotor sensations. The individual automatically reacts to these sensations.

To recall such a memory is to re-experience the physical sensations and reflexive bodily movements that we experienced during the original, memory-forming event. This kind of memory is dispositional or implicit memory.

Henderson says that our entire adult emotional life, our ability to spontaneously experience pleasant and painful feelings and emotions, is built upon the contents of these sensorimotor memories. Throughout my book I refer to this early memory system as either the *amygdalic memory system* or the *primal memory system*.

Henderson goes on to theorize that this memory system ceases its function upon the maturation of a second, more sophisticated memory system. This transition from a primitive to a sophisticated memory system occurs during the fifth or sixth year, when the myelinization of the hippocampal structure of the brain is complete. Thereafter, all memories are encoded as feeling-neutral, visual representations. Furthermore, these more sophisticated memories automatically gain access to the logic functions of the left hemisphere of our brain, once the corpus callosum is fully myelinated. This occurs at around age ten.

I refer to this mature memory system as the *hippocampal memory system*. If an individual recalls a hippocampal memory, and it does bring up a feeling or sensation, it is because it is connected to one or more of these earlier kinds of memories (they both share a common feeling). Henderson thinks that once the hippocampal memory system is fully functional, the amygdalic memory system becomes an artifact, functioning only as a repository for very early, sensorimotor and emotional memories.

My studies have led me to speculate that the amygdalic memory system continues to be active in memory formation after the maturation of the hippocampal memory system, but only as a protective device: one which functions to guard developing self-awareness against the ongoing disintegrative potential of traumatic life experiences.

A *primal memory* is any memory that the amygdalic memory system has encoded. That is, the memory is made by the first (or primal) memory system. If it is encoded prior to the maturation of the hippocampal system it may be either a pleasant memory or a fear memory (because this is the only means of encoding experience). If it is formed after the maturation of the hippocampal system, it will be (exclusively) a fear memory.

MEMORY STORAGE

One theory of how memory is recorded states that all incoming information to the nervous system is electrical in nature. So-called short-term memory may be temporarily encoded on this level (as a certain electrical configuration within the brain). Then somehow, the electrical impulses within the nerve circuitry stimulate the DNA inside each nerve cell. As a result of this stimulus DNA sends RNA out into the cell with a message to construct specific protein memory molecules, usually on the cell's surface. This newly formed protein in some way stores a long-term memory that is subject to recall.[5] Recent studies in fear memory retrieval reinforce this theory.

In addition to being able to store experience, the nervous system operates such that we can associate and generalize these experiences. Because of this functional ability, we are able to automatically draw upon our previous experiences each time we are presented with a present-day challenge. That is, whenever a present event feels like a past pleasant or painful situation, we automatically generate a pleasure or fear response. These automatic responses enable us to have the phenomenological experience of an emotional life. It also has survival value because we do not have to learn over and over again to avoid dangerous experiences. That is, we learn how to automatically react in fear to any present event that feels like the original fear-provoking event. For example, if one is bitten by a snake, one may automatically react with a fear response when suddenly spying a coiled rope on the ground later in life. One associates the original experience with a certain feeling and generalizes the original response onto same-feeling events in the present.

This natural, brain capability (memory storage and automatic recall) is a double-edged sword. Whenever someone triggers pleasant primal memories, the person recalling these memories automatically re-experiences the sensations and emotions that are associated with love, nurture, empathy, etc. This person experiences what we like to refer to as our "human" qualities. In the same way, whenever someone triggers painful primal memories, the person recalling these memories automatically re-experiences painful sensations and emotions that are associated with fear, hatred, envy, selfishness, anger, and other such emotions.

The automatic reexperiencing of fear-related primal memories is the necessary condition of neurosis. And the present-day experience that triggers those memories, is the sufficient condition.

Joseph LeDoux's research supports Henderson's speculations about the existence of multiple memory systems. In his discussion of the differences between implicit and explicit memory he says:

> The conscious memory of the past experience and the physiological responses elicited thus reflect the operation of two separate memory systems that operate in parallel. Only by taking these systems apart in the brain have neuroscientists been able to figure out that these are different kinds of memory rather than one memory with multiple forms of expression. The work of our lab has been focused on the neural system underlying the formation of implicit emotional memories.[6]

Amygdalic memories are LeDoux's implicit memories. And his explicit memories are hippocampal or declarative memories.

A discussion of Janov's imprints is frustrated by the fact that most people understand memory only in terms of conceptual or declarative memories. It is generally understood that to remember something is to hold a visual representation up before the mind's eye. We tend not to think of a recalled, nonconceptual, sensory experience as a memory. Therefore, it is helpful to think of pleasant and painful primal memories as conditioned, pleasure and fear responses.

Human beings have had to evolve in a world in which painful, disruptive events threaten existence. This reality is reflected in the development of mechanisms of pain repression very early on in evolution. In order for human evolution to progress, it is clear that present-occurring perception or awareness of pain must have had to be dampened, yet remembered, so that future painful events could be avoided. This kind of capability would grant a survival advantage. This reactive response would have had to evolve very early on in the development of life on earth. Otherwise, how could living systems have overcome the disintegrative, environmental elements in the very early stages of development? And, if McLean's model of evolutionary brain development is correct, in mammals this function would be located deep down in the primitive neural structure of the brain.[7] This type of brain function would necessarily have to be linked to sensations or feeling states, rather than to rational thought processes. And, in fact, present life experience is still initially processed through early brain structure.[8]

When one contemplates the many so-called reflex functions, such as removing a finger from a hot object or blinking whenever an object approaches the eye, it is clear that these things happen without the participation of conscious awareness. But it is also clear that some form of consciousness must exist below the level of awareness, which automatically protects the body from cellular damage. Arthur Janov has labeled this function: *first line consciousness.*

Similarly, and for the very same logical reasons, the evolution of human self-awareness must have required the simultaneous evolution of a protective mechanism that guarded against its disintegration.

As a species and throughout each individual's life span, the sense of self must be slowly constructed out of life experience. Modern biological theory acknowledges that the classical nature-versus-nurture theory of human development is naive. It is now believed that genetic structure unfolds and is subsequently modified by its interaction with the quality of the environment with which it comes into contact.[9] Genetically programmed nerve cell sprouting and pruning present a good example of this reality.

According to evolution theory, nature adapts existing structures to the introduction of novel survival challenges. An example of this is the foot. The foot did not evolve for the purpose of movement on land. Rather, an existing structure, as used in a novel way to permit land movement. The fin's continual use in this way brought the foot into existence.

Did nature utilize an existing brain structure in a novel way, to protect the newly emerging function of self-awareness from disintegration? I think that it did. That structure is the primitive amygdalic memory system. And this adaptation, while it assisted the evolution of self-awareness, simultaneously precipitated the necessary condition for the dissociative function, as well as the condition of fear memory intrusion that is associated with post-traumatic stress disorder.

Van der Kolk suggests that the amygdalic memory system may become activated in the case of traumatic experiences.[10] This memory system becomes activated by highly charged, emotional experiences, which threaten to be disruptive of higher-order human consciousness. And, simultaneously, the experience is prevented from being recorded in hippocampal memory by the presence of high levels of cortisol, which are a result of the highly stressful nature of the traumatic experience. Van der Kolk feels that this process is the essence of dissociation.

By simultaneously shunting traumatic experience into amygdalic memory, while disabling hippocampal memory formation, the sensorimotor and emotional components of traumatic experience are "imprinted," while higher-order consciousness is preserved.

Our bodies absorb the "blows" of traumatic experience in order to preserve the integrity of our ability to be self-aware.

For example, a woman might have no conceptual memory of having been raped—think of what it would be like to wake up every morning with a vivid conceptual memory of a rape experience, yet she can no longer tolerate intimacy with men because a man's touch "feels" frightening or uncomfortable. That is, it triggers a fear response (a painful primal memory), rather than a pleasure response. Her dissociated body memory of one man's abusive treatment of her has become generalized onto all men.

The activation of the amygdalic memory system in the event of traumatic experience is an example of nature's adaptation of existing structure (the amygdalic memory system) to novel experience (the evolution of the ability to be self-aware).

There is, however, a problem inherent in this adaptation. The use of amygdalic memory to record traumatic experience represents an encapsulating event. In other words, this process effectively prevents the integration of the memory of the traumatic experience into the whole psychic structure.

The term "psychic structure" describes the felt sense of having an enduring existence (sense of past, present, and future), which is made possible by the existence of the left-hemisphere, frontal area of the brain, which analyzes an experience and associates it with other knowledge within a time matrix. This activity, coupled with hippocampal or declarative memory, which can be consciously recalled and reflected upon, gives us our sense of having a personal history.

On the cellular level, a process called phagocytosis has evolved as a defense mechanism. For example, when the body recognizes an invading bacterium as being capable of disintegrating cellular integrity, a white blood cell moves to the site, engulfs the harmful material within its body by trapping it in a section of the cell's plasma membrane, and then pinches that membrane off inside of the cell. The bacterium is thus encapsulated from the rest of the body cells. Later, the bacterium is fused with a lysosome and is destroyed. Ultimately, the body expels the destroyed bacterium via the organs of elimination.

Likewise, *dissociation*, the automatic shunting of a traumatic experience into the amygdalic or primal memory system and its simultaneous blockage from high-order brain function and hippocampal memory formation, can be seen as the first step in a detoxification process: the neuro-cellular identification of a disintegrative event and its encapsulation.

To recall a primal memory is to re-experience the body sensations that were present during the original painful experience. It is important to understand that retrieved primal memories directly stimulate the functioning of the autonomic nervous system, just as the original memory-forming event stimulated this system. That is, the autonomic nervous system cannot differentiate between a present threat (physical) and a recalled threat (psychological). This is consistent with mind/body identity theory. If the original, fear experience produced a rapid heartbeat, for example, the recollected memory *is* rapid heartbeat. If the original experience produced shortness of breath, the recollected memory *is* shortness of breath. This is evident in the situation in which one is called upon to speak in front of an audience and suddenly experiences heart palpitations and shortness of breath. If one asks oneself what the audience is doing to cause the heart to beat faster or to cause the breath to shorten, it becomes obvious that the audience cannot be causing this autonomic response. Rather, the response is being self-generated. The self-generated response is a recalled primal memory of an earlier experience that had the same feeling as the present experience. Something about the feeling of the present experience is triggering the recollection of a primal memory.

If it is true that constant imprint intrusion is the cause of neurosis and that the intrusion has a direct effect upon the autonomic nervous system, then the healing of neurosis should be objectively demonstrable by the direct measurement in changes of autonomic functioning prior to and after therapy. Janov has demonstrated this, as well as changes in brain function. A discussion of his evidence will occur later in this book.

MEMORY RETRIEVAL

In order for information to be saved in a computer, it must be assigned a name so that it can be retrieved (distinguished from other information) at a later date. The "save as" function is used to accomplish this. Whenever one needs to retrieve information, one enters the name into the computer. This brings up the information that exists in that named file. This information is, thus, made available for consideration.

The human memory system seems to work in a similar way, except that there is no search name. There is, instead, a search feeling. Because it is initially processed through primitive brain structure, memories of human experience are labeled with feelings. Each past experience had a particular feeling attached to it. And when the brain encoded this experience, it used this feeling, just as a computer uses a "search name." Likewise, each present-day experience has a certain feeling to it. When the present feeling is experienced, it is like entering a search name into a computer. This feeling automatically brings up memories that have been tagged with this similar feeling. In this way the present experience automatically accesses relevant past experience. Note the difference in human memory retrieval: a feeling is a more general entity than is a word. With a computer there can be only one file assigned to one name. In the brain, multiple memories can be assigned to a feeling. This creates the possibility for what Janov has termed a "chain of pain." This chain is a network of fear memories that share a common feeling. The human brain associates memories with one another, based upon shared, common feelings.

Additionally, LeDoux suggests that memories of our experiences are fixed by the intensity of the feeling associated with the experience.[11] So, the more emotionally charged an experience is, the more likely it is that it will be encoded as a fear memory. This is because strong emotions usually signify that something needs to be attended to (for survival).

His research demonstrates that memory is malleable when it is first encoded and also during each recollection.

> "New" memories are initially labile and sensitive to disruption before being consolidated into stable long-term memories. Much evidence indicates that this consolidation involves the synthesis of new proteins in neurons. The lateral and basal nuclei of the amygdala (LBA) are believed to be a site of memory storage in fear learning. Infusion of the protein synthesis inhibitor anisomycin into the LBA shortly after training prevents consolidation of fear memories. Here we show that consolidated fear memories, when reactivated during retrieval, return to a labile state in which infusion of anisomycin shortly after memory reactivation produces amnesia on later tests, regardless of whether reactivation was performed 1 or 14 days after conditioning. The same treatment of anisomycin, in the absence of memory reactivation left memory intact. Consistent with a time-limited role for protein synthesis production in consolidation, delay of the infusion until six hours after memory reactivation produced no amnesia. Our data show that consolidated fear memories, when reactivated, return to a labile state that requires de novo protein synthesis for reconsolidation. These findings are not predicted by traditional theories of memory consolidation.[12]

So, in order for a memory to be recollected, the protein molecules on which that memory is encoded must first be disassembled. Afterward, new molecules must be made, resulting in the re-storage of the recalled memory onto the new molecule chain. LeDoux's experiments suggest that the process of protein reassembly takes six hours. Because the newly "disembodied" memory is labile (during its recollection), if new information is added during this six hour period, this new information may become part of the restored memory, thereby making a slightly different memory than had existed prior to the recollection. This process of memory-making goes to the very heart of the false-memory debate. It also is critically important to the emotional healing process. It explains why activities such as repatterning, re-parenting, and rebirthing, can have therapeutic value.

Just because someone has a memory of abuse and really believes that it happened, does not necessarily mean this memory be trusted. The current memory formation and retrieval research suggests that if that memory has been repeatedly recalled and manipulated, there is room for doubt. I believe that the false-memory argument is confused. The confusion exists because of a failure to acknowledge the essential difference between dispositional (fear) memories and contextual memories. While both sets of memories are encoded and recalled, they are recalled *differently*.

One must remember that a fear memory is an encapsulated memory. It is encapsulated in the sense that it has not been integrated within the larger set of contextual memories. One cannot construct a story about fear memories. They are something that just happen, over and over. They are a conditioned response and happen as body reactions, alterations in the autonomic nervous system.

Because they are separated from the contextual memory-making process, they are separated from the sensory data (of current experience) that is continually informing that system. Additionally, they do not have access to the logic structures of the brain.

A recalled contextual memory is bombarded with new data within a time matrix. A recalled fear memory is not.

And yet, LeDoux's work demonstrates that fear memory is also labile after it is recalled. This presents the possibility that it might become modified. Indeed, his experiments show that fear memory can be eradicated chemically in animals upon its reactivation.

A recalled primal memory is always true, in the sense that it is a re-representation of the sensations and emotions that the person experienced during the original trauma. It is a direct, autonomic response and, hence, cannot be false. The conceptualization that it was his mom or dad that did the abusing will be accurate to the extent that the hippocampal memory-making process was able to create a declarative memory of the event while it was happening. Because the extent of dissociation is dependent upon the amount of stress involved, as well as the amount of control that the abused individual senses that he has while being traumatized, it is possible that the primal memory may be completely devoid of conceptual memory or it may be linked to fragments of conceptual memory. These variables make it possible for traumatic memories to exist on a continuum (from no visual representation to some visual representation). In other words, the abused may recollect only painful sensations and body reactions or he may have actual fragments of conceptual memories of it being his mom or dad. This is obviously very error-fraught territory.

Thus one task of a defense attorney in a case in which abuse is being alleged would be the establishment of whether or not the accuser's memories may have been implanted at a later date.

Janov believes that the imprint is an extremely durable memory. In fact, he believes that once the primal memory is formed, it exists forever in the body in its original, pristine state. No matter how many times it is recalled, the imprint gets restored in its original, unmodified state. Only primalling the memory is able to modify the structure of an imprint. He calls this process "feeling the feeling." A discussion of the term "primalling" will be presented later on in the book.

What is it like to relive a traumatic experience? Since film is primarily a visual medium, motion pictures have given a false impression of what it is like to relive a traumatic event. In movies of this sort there is always an epiphany in which a coherent, declarative memory of the traumatic experience of the past finally rises, full-blown, into the consciousness of the traumatized person. The person visualizes the traumatic event and, once this happens, he remembers and resolves the event. This process is clearly depicted in the movie *Prince of Tides*. This presupposes a model of repression in which the mind actually records a coherent, explicit memory of the traumatic event and then throws up a screen that blocks these memories from reaching conscious awareness. Lower the screen and the memory emerges.

If Bessell van der Kolk is correct about the mechanism of dissociation of traumatic events, the reliving of a traumatic event would be substantially different than this cinematic portrayal. My own traumatic memory retrieval experiences confirm this difference.

According to van der Kolk, the declarative memory-making process is disabled during a traumatic experience. That is, the brain is incapable of making a coherent declarative memory during a traumatizing event or, to the extent that it does, it is fragmented, containing bits and pieces of what happened prior to, during, or after the event. What does happen is that the emotional and sensorimotor component of the experience is encoded in primal memory. Since no coherent declarative memory is encoded in the first place, there can obviously be no coherent declarative recollection of the event, unlike the depiction in the movies. What are subject to recall are the somatic elements (the sensorimotor reactions) that originally occurred during the trauma. And, if fragmentary elements of declarative memory exist, they, too, are subject to recall. The emergence of fragments of declarative memories of a traumatic event have been referred to as flashbulb memories. A piece of visualization emerges abruptly "out of the darkness," as though someone took a picture with a flash.

This is precisely what happened to me during the course of my personal experience with primal therapy and the retrieval of a central traumatic event.

It is Van der Kolk's observation that:

> Memories of trauma tend to, at least initially, be predominantly experienced as fragments of the sensory components of the event: as visual images, olfactory, auditory, or kinesthetic sensations, or intense waves of feelings (which patients usually claim to be representations of elements of the original traumatic event). What is intriguing is that patients consistently claim that their perceptions are exact representations of sensations at the time of the trauma.[13]

And:

> The highly elevated physiological responses that accompany the recall of traumatic experiences that happened years, and sometimes decades before, illustrate the intensity and timelessness with which traumatic memories continue to affect current experience.[14]

Janov has this to say about the retrieval of an imprint or primal memory: "The human system has the remarkable innate capacity to return to the exact body and brain state originally present in the trauma, not to think about it or imagine it, but to replicate it exactly."[15]

LeDoux has demonstrated that the human memory system encodes normal memories and traumatic memories in very different ways. Van der Kolk has this to say about the difference:

> We have known since the final decades of the 19th century that extreme fear, terror, and helplessness during a traumatic event can overwhelm people's biological and psychological adaptive mechanisms. They are unable to assimilate and integrate their experience. Their "implicit" (sensory and emotional) memories of the trauma are "dissociated" and return not as ordinary memories of what happened, but as intense emotional reactions, nightmares, horrifying images, aggressive behavior, physical pain, and bodily states. The mental imprints of the trauma return.[16]

I have concluded that Janov's imprints are actually implicit fear memories of the kind that van der Kolk is describing. The cluster of symptoms, which are exhibited by people who have suffered traumatic experience, are a compilation of that person's unique reaction to the autonomic response that is triggered by the fear memory intrusion. And the various symptom clusters are referred to, collectively, as post traumatic stress disorder.

Van der Kolk says that:

> The core pathology of PTSD is that certain sensations or emotions
> related to traumatic experiences are dissociated, keep returning in
> unbidden ways, and do not fade with time. It is normal to distort one's
> memories over the years, but people with PTSD seem unable to put an
> event behind them or to minimize its impact.[17]

And:

> Traumatized people rarely realize that their intense feelings and reac-
> tions are based on past experience. They blame their present surround-
> ings for the way they feel and thereby rationalize their feelings. The
> almost infinite capacity to rationalize in this way keeps them from hav-
> ing to confront the helplessness and horror of their past; they are pro-
> tected from becoming aware of the true meaning of the messages they
> receive from the brain areas that specialize in self-preservation and
> detection of danger.[18]

Janov states that neurotic behavior is caused by the constant intrusion of the
imprint into everyday experiences. I have equated Janov's imprints with fear
memories. Therefore, if my assumptions are correct, it can be concluded that
what Janov was describing as neurosis thirty years ago is identical to what is now
being termed PTSD. In other words, neurosis *is* post traumatic stress disorder.

If this is true, one can now understand why Janov adamantly insists that conventional "talk therapies" are not able to cure neurosis.

Again, van der Kolk (describing fear memories) says:

> These emotionally labeled sensations are believed to be indelible or at
> least extraordinarily difficult to extinguish. Once the amygdala is pro-
> grammed to remember particular sounds, smells, and bodily sensations
> as dangerous, a person is likely always to respond to these stimuli as a
> trigger for fight or flight reactions.[19]

Conventional psychotherapy relies on top-down processing, which inhibits rather
than integrates unpleasant sensations and emotions.

> In traditional insight-oriented psychotherapy, people can grasp that cer-
> tain emotional or somatic reactions belong to the past and are irrelevant
> to their lives today. This may help them override automatic physiologi-

cal responses to traumatic reminders, although it will not abolish them. It provides a deeper understanding of why they feel the way they do, but insight of this nature is unlikely to be capable of reconfiguring the over-active alarm systems of the brain.[20]

In other words, understanding why one is acting neurotically cannot remove the ability to recall and to reenact painful emotional memories. Or, as Janov says: you cannot reason away the pain of your imprint. It is now understood that the rational thought process is incapable of reconfiguring the brain's alarm system.

Hence, with a rational mind one can do many things to modify behavior (providing resistance to the flow of primal memory), but the imprinted primal memory remains, still loaded with the energy of the original experience, still waiting to emerge. Like water, it will find the path of least resistance, and then it will flow forth once again. An example of this is seen every time someone gives up cigarettes, only to begin overeating and gaining weight. Smoking may be a learned repetitive behavior, which helps to keep painful primal memories from intruding into awareness. When one decides to stop smoking, excessive eating accomplishes the same thing!

A neurobiological reality works against a top down approach to the treatment of neurosis:

> Neuroanatomists have shown that the pathways that connect the emotional processing system of fear, the amygdala, with the thinking brain, the neocortex are not symmetrical—the connections from the cortex to the amygdala are considerably weaker than those from the amygdala to the cortex. This may explain why, once an emotion is aroused, it is so hard for us to turn it off at will. The asymmetry of these connections may also help us understand why psychotherapy is often such a difficult and prolonged process—it relies on imperfect channels of communication between brain systems involved in cognition and emotion.[21]

It follows, then, that what is required for the healing of neurosis is the type of facilitation that helps to reconfigure the overactive alarm system of the brain.

Janov claims that the therapeutic techniques of primal therapy cure neurosis. His techniques work to eliminate many of the symptoms of neurosis by addressing the cause of the symptoms: the imprint. But, unfortunately, he does not make these techniques known to the general public. Today he still operates his own therapy center and teaches his techniques exclusively to his students; furthermore, he steadfastly refuses to acknowledge anyone else's work (that is, anyone who was not trained by him) as being useful in the eradication of neurosis. He has written many books over a period of thirty years and is continuing to author more. However, a search for references to Janov's work within the psychotherapeutic community reveals nothing. This community has overtly ignored thirty years of his research. Yet, it is apparent (from the study of van der Kolk's works, for example) that this same community has been absorbing his ideas and advancing them within the emerging field of trauma therapy.

MEMORY AND STRESS

It has been known for a long time that stress interferes with the proper processing of declarative memory. When presented with a stressful situation, the activation of the hypothalamic-pituitary-adrenal (HPA) axis stimulates the adrenal glands to manufacture excess cortisol, a catabolic hormone, which, in effect, causes the augmented breakdown of body tissue in order to release more energy for the defensive needs of a threatened body. When excess cortisol infuses neural tissue, it interferes with the conceptual memory and decision-making process. Additionally, blood flow is restricted in the frontal parts of the brain and is shunted to brainstem (survival) structures.

According to van der Kolk, it takes a special set of circumstances to disable the hippocampal memory system. Not only must a situation be highly stressful and emotionally charged, but also the person enduring the trauma must feel helpless to change the outcome of the traumatic event.

Janov had this to say over thirty years ago: "Overload" is not simply a matter of how traumatic the stimulus is; on an internal level it must be a stimulus for which "there is no option for escape."[22] Hence, both men believe that a shutdown occurs when there is a painful and uncontrollable sensory overload. It is an automatic brain process—a defense.

So, when these two conditions occur together within a person's experience, the hippocampal system "blinks." A record of the physical and emotional reaction to this traumatic event is encoded, but its visual representation within the hippocampal memory system is not. It is important to understand that the phrases "highly stressful" and "helpless to change the outcome," the two presumed variables of fear memory processing, exist on a continuum. They may be conditioned by an individual's genetic disposition, as well as age factors. The extent of the visual representation is dependent upon the cortisol level, which is dependent upon the level of stress and the level of helplessness that the person feels. The person thereby automatically dissociates himself from the fearful event on a continuum that extends from having some declarative memory of the event to having none at all. In this way the person can endure and survive the traumatic event in which he is helpless to change the outcome: an automatic fear response (memory) is created as a survival mechanism for future reference, and the integrity of the self-awareness function is preserved.

> Dissociation [of a traumatic experience] refers to a compartmentalization of experience: elements of the experience are not integrated into a unitary whole, but are stored in memory as isolated fragments and stored as sensory perceptions, affective states or as behavioral reenactments. While dissociation may temporarily serve an adaptive function, in the long range, lack of integration of traumatic memories seems to be the critical element that leads to the development of the complex behavioral change that we call Post traumatic Stress Disorder. Intense arousal seems to interfere with proper information processing and the storage of information into narrative (explicit) memory.[23]

The implication is that an integration of these traumatic memories would heal PTSD. Janov's use of the term "primal" is a description of a therapeutic process whereby traumatic memories can be integrated into the whole psychic structure.

THE CONTINUUM OF PTSD

Bessell van der Kolk's research with PTSD involves cases of dramatic incidents of child abuse, rape, or terror (of the type that soldiers experience in combat). The impression one gets is that traumatic memory-making is connected to an on/off switch, and that an experience must reach a critical level in order to be dissociated. I think that fear memory-making is connected to a rheostat. That is, there is a gradient of dissociation involved in all experiences that are capable of disrupting the self-awareness function. If it is the case that the process of dissociation is distributed on a continuum, does this not imply that there can be different levels of PTSD? I believe that neurosis exists on a continuum that is directly related to the level of stress associated with the traumatic event and the level of control the person believes he has over the event. What the conventional psychotherapeutic community is referring to as PTSD is merely neurotic behavior at its extreme pole. At one end of the spectrum is the person whose mild fear memory intrusion is preventing him from establishing a loving relationship with his mate. At the opposite end of the spectrum is the person whose severe fear memory intrusion has resulted in dissociative identity disorder.

Rape is a traumatic event. But so is being a sensitive young boy who is always being picked on for being a "little girl." So is being a young child and being continually told that you are stupid or bad. So is the experience of a "fat" or "skinny" person who desperately seeks approval by a social group, who, instead, is continually and openly humiliated by the group. So is the child who is a victim of bullying in the school environment. While there is a difference in the intensity of these events, there is no difference in kind with regard to how the brain processes these events. In all cases, the person's, fragile, developing sense of "self" is being assaulted by a disintegrative event. A thoughtful recollection of one's childhood will lead to the realization that every young child's environment is filled with events that have the potential to disintegrate the developing sense of self. Even in what is referred to as a normal childhood, the continuity of self-awareness is continually being threatened and must be preserved in some way. The process of dissociation is the protective mechanism. The intensity of the dissociation determines the intensity of the neurosis. And, all human beings exist somewhere along that continuum.

What Janov has been saying for over thirty years is that all neurosis is trauma-related and must be treated accordingly. Where his views of trauma differ from van der Kolk and others is in the domain of traumatic occurrences.

Janov believes that people can experience and encode trauma beginning in the twenty-sixth week of fetal development. Thereafter, all painful experiences in the womb are traumatic. An unfavorable birth experience is traumatic. An unfavorable early life environment is traumatic. He believes that imprinting (encoding of traumatic memories) is curtailed at around age ten; however, I believe that it continues throughout life and not only in the case of extreme trauma.

Again, Van der Kolk's work seems to imply that imprinting occurs in an on/off fashion during highly traumatic experience. I am suggesting that it occurs in a rheostatted fashion, during any event that has the potential of disrupting the continuity of one's self-awareness. Remember, the disabling of the hippocampal and neocortical structures occurs because of a high level of cortisol, which is a direct effect of a highly stressful event. There is no mechanical on/off switch. Rather, there is a continuous rising of a disruptive hormone. So, it would seem logical that higher cortical function might be disrupted in a progressive way.

PRIMAL MEMORIES GENERATE PSYCHO-NEUROLOGICAL IMBALANCES

Baker has this to say about the study of illness in general:

> The theory, if you can call it that, that has dominated medical science for 70 years is that people get sick because they are the victims of disease entities. A better theory, in my opinion, is that people get sick because of a disruption of the dynamic balance that exists between themselves and their environment.[24]

One can apply Baker's general health theory to the process of emotional health.

Sound emotional health requires a balanced and accurate response of the nervous system to environmental stimuli. This is accomplished through the action of the autonomic nervous system. This part of the nervous system reacts to its environment in two equal but opposite ways. One set of responses is initiated when one encounters a need to be protected from something. This is called the sympathetic response. When this system is activated all of the body functions are sequestered for the purpose of allowing the body to either defend itself against the threat or to run away from it. This process involves flooding the system with stress hormones, whose catabolic effect upon body cells fuels the heightened fight, flight, or freeze responses.

After the threat is dealt with, the body returns to its parasympathetic mode, in which the body processes are relaxed and can begin to repair from the effects of this heightened state of arousal. One of the mechanisms of the parasympathetic response is crying. Frey's research has proven that emotional crying is a detoxifying process whereby the body gets rid of the stress producing hormones left over from the sympathetic discharge.[25]

Because the nervous system is continually adapting to a highly variable environment, the life process reflects a constant cycle of sympathetic and parasympathetic responses. And, when they are working in a balanced way, these autonomic responses enable one to live in a healthy (balanced) emotional and physical state. In order to function properly, in either the sympathetic or parasympathetic modes, proper responses to the stimuli of each mode must be allowed to occur.

It is quite natural to get angry and to freeze, fight against, or run away from real, threatening events. And it is quite natural to cry after the threat is removed. That is how the body readjusts its equilibrium after a frightening encounter. But, when these heightened responses occur spontaneously without the presence of an actual threatening event, we are acting neurotically.

The process of socialization has interfered with this natural cycle. This natural, self-balancing system gets disturbed very early in life. Poor parental attachment behavior during the first nine months disturbs this balancing mechanism. Later on, parents begin teaching the child how to defeat these normal responses. They do this by ignoring, punishing, or shaming the child. Rarely do they take the time necessary to witness and contain what they perceive as unwanted behavior. Rarely do they allow the natural progression of this autonomic response.

According to Solter:

> Not all crying is an indication of an immediate need or want. Much of it is a natural stress-release mechanism that allows children to heal from the effects of frightening or frustrating experiences that have occurred previously. Children use tears and tantrums to resolve trauma and release tensions. It is therefore not the caretaker's job to stop the crying or raging, because these behaviors are, in themselves, basic needs from birth on.
>
> [And] [i]t is best if babies and children who cry are never ignored. Their cries should always receive a nurturing response.[26]

Instead of this nurturing response, our parents tend to treat our anger and tears as annoyingly primitive, unpleasant behaviors, which must be ignored, shamed, or threatened out of us as soon as possible.

Because of a failure on the part of parents to see their child's anger/crying cycle as a natural homeostatic mechanism, children develop "a disruption of the dynamic balance that exists between themselves and their environment."

HUMAN DEVELOPMENT AND THE ROOTS OF NEUROSIS

In order to properly understand Janov, it is necessary to have an ecological concept of human development. All living things emerge out of, and grow into, an environment that is continuously flowing through them like a silent, invisible tide. As the environment flows, every one of the trillions of cells that make up the individual actively captures and integrates the elements of the environment that it needs to maintain life and health. This process is called nutrition. In the process of doing this, byproducts of this interaction are generated that can threaten the integrity of the cell. Additionally, dangerous substances enter the body, and the body takes in substances in excess of that which it can process. Therefore, the body also tries to isolate these threatening and/or excessive elements and return them to the environment. This process is called detoxification. The continued existence and maintenance of the health of our internal environment is achieved when there is a balance between these processes. The process of detoxification, of protecting the living cell from disintegrating events, is so critical to the life process that up to 80 percent of the body's daily energy expenditure is used to accomplish this.[27] To the extent that this balance is disturbed, one experiences this disequilibrium as "illness." This is the way that a naturopath understands health and sickness.

Our first environment is mother's womb. This is where all mammals begin their emergence from the energy field. And, with the exception of certain substances that cannot cross the placental barrier, mother's environment flows through the fetus like a silent, invisible tide. During this time, the elements of this environment are captured and integrated into the fetus's cellular structure. The fetus returns the byproducts of this integrative process back to mother, who returns it to the general environment. Mother's emotional reactions to her environment exist as flows of chemicals, such as hormones. So, in a very real sense, mother's physical and emotional experience during pregnancy is also the fetus's experience.

The sensations that the fetus experiences in response to this environment can be either pleasant or painful, depending upon whether the environment is nurturing to its growth or antagonistic to it. These experiences are entered into primal memory as either pleasant or painful sensorimotor data. This is the only type of memory-making that exists at this point of our development.

The primal memory system is recording our intrauterine experiences and the experiences during the first six years of our lives in terms of these physical sensations and emotions.

To recall such a memory later on in life is to re-experience the pleasant or painful sensations.

This primitive memory system is a function of the right hemisphere of the brain and is in operation well before the myelinization of the corpus callosum. This is a structure that connects the left and right hemispheres of the brain. Because of the early disconnection with the left-hemisphere, amygdalic memories are uninformed by left-hemisphere logic functions, such as time sequencing. In the right hemisphere, the time is always now. It is the left hemisphere that enables us to have a sense of the past. Because of this, a recalled primal memory has the urgency associated with the present. It feels like it is happening now. And it is, in a sense, because the physical sensations are happening now and are triggering the same sympathetic response within the body as did the original fearful experience. This lack of connection to left-hemisphere functions, this lack of time-contextualizing, enables one to mistake present experience as being the cause of the recalled uncomfortable feelings.

Human beings are born prematurely. This is necessitated by the evolution of the very large brain. Because of its size and rapid growth, if human babies are not delivered within nine months, their heads would be too large to pass through the birth canal. Because of this, the child is delivered only partially developed and thus completely dependent upon its caregivers for its very existence. Human beings are, in effect, still in the fetal stage of their development during the first nine months <u>after</u> birth. It takes another nine months of development before crawling enables the child to begin its ability to remove itself from dangerous situations. Therefore, the child is as helpless and dependent during the first nine months after its birth as it was during its womb life. Additionally, its brain is still in the process of wiring itself. Indeed, it is not until the fifth and tenth years, respectively, that the hippocampal and corpus callosum structures of the brain are fully myelinated.

Thus, Montague urges the viewing of the human gestation period as being eighteen, rather than nine, months.[28] And John Bowlby feels that continual holding and mirroring of the child's expressions (for the nine months after birth) is absolutely necessary for the proper emotional development of a child. And, indeed, work by Schore and other modern attachment-oriented researchers demonstrates that the frontal structures of the child's brain, responsible for impulse control, are severely compromised by the lack of proper parental attentiveness during this early period.[29] The brain actually prunes away important nerve cells in this area, in response to faulty parenting.

During the first nine months after its birth, a child has a biological drive to have contact or at least close proximity to its mother when in need. Bowlby calls this drive "attachment."

He feels that separation from mother is developmentally disastrous for the child because it interferes with the child's instinctual needs during this time.

If the child is in need, in pain, is frightened, or startled it will instinctively behave in ways that elicit closeness (eye contact, smiles, crying, clinging) from the mother. This he calls "attachment behavior." The mother's attentive response to the child's instinctive behavior gives the child the other half of (the environmental component of) what it needs to cope with the experience.

So, the mother's mirroring and touch during this phase of development are forms of nutrition, just as are food and drink. Not only is the mother's responsive behavior a nutrient, it is also an essential nutrient. Just as the body cannot achieve proper physical structure without the availability of essential nutrients, the mind cannot achieve proper psychic structure without the availability to the child of its mother's essential attachment input. The quality of this nutrition can be rich or poor. The child's emotional development will be robust or stunted depending upon the nutritional content of the mother's attention. The mother's responses to the child's attachment behavior during this critical period of development form the template for the child's future responses to the world. Since the child records its experiences as sensorimotor data during this time, poor attachment behavior on the part of the mother results in the child's inability to process its fearful experiences. This, in turn, results in dissociation and the formation of a pool of painful primal memories within the child.

If the parent consistently behaves in a way that is qualitatively responsive to the child's attachment behavior, the child will develop a secure relationship or attachment style. To the extent that the parent fails to mirror (or attend to) its child's attachment behavior, the child will develop an ambivalent or avoidant relationship with its mother.

The mother's failure to adequately attend to the child's attachment behavior is a failure to provide the "essential nutrients" necessary for the child to process its stressful experiences. This lack of nutrition is highly stressful for the child. It is not getting what it needs from its environment to properly process its distressing experience. So it begins to dissociate from this experience. And a fear memory is created and stored.

One can think of the mother and child relationship as being symbiotic. It is simply nature's way of extending the womb relationship. Whereas the child's needs are met through the umbilical cord and placenta during the first nine months, its needs during the second nine months are met through the synchronous need/need fulfillment relationship of the mother and child. The child's attachment behavior and the mother's synchronous response is nature's way of extending or continuing the placental relationship. In fact, it is interesting to note that the placenta itself is an organ that is made up of the tissue of both the fetus and the mother. Here is a good example of what is meant by the phrase "the organism and its environment are a single entity." From the moment of conception, through the child's nine months after birth, the mother and child are to be seen as a single functional unit: the mother-child dyad. The research of attachment theorists is revealing that, with regard to the proper brain and emotional development of the child, that dyad is an inseparable, mini-environment.

The child's attachment behavior is instinctual. It is not clear whether the human parent's response behavior is instinctual (but subject to modification by experience) or learned. In either case, this means that a mother can fail to fulfill her half of the symbiotic relationship.

If the symbiotic relationship is properly established, the child will "develop good cause/effect thinking, feels powerful, trusts others, shows exploratory behavior, develops empathy and a conscience."[30] In other words, the child grows out into its environment, which it experiences as pleasant, just as a plant is attracted to the warm rays of the sun. In this case, the infant's pool of primal memories is being loaded with pleasant sensorimotor data, which will be continually re-experienced and projected into the world throughout its life. Life generally feels safe and good. This is referred to as a secure attachment.

If this relationship is faulty, the child begins to develop mistrust and shuts down attachment behavior. A faulty symbiotic relationship can create avoidant attachment, in which the child begins to avoid the parent (lack of eye contact, turning away, etc). In other words, the child retreats from its environment, which it experiences as painful, just as any living thing retracts from a painful stimulus.

> The attachment-challenged child, because it lacks the support necessary to process its stressful experiences, becomes overwhelmed by stressful experiences, dissociates from them, and begins its lifelong reaction to the fear memory or imprint of its frightening, unprocessed experiences.

Thereafter, the child chronically links a prior fear reaction with present activity. This manifests itself in a resistant/ambivalent attachment, in which the child either passively or actively shows hostility toward the parent. The parent has become a trigger for the infant's fear memory retrieval. And, because the brain has the ability to associate and generalize its experiences, this early behavior translates into similar relationship behavior when the child becomes an adult. In this case, the attachment-disordered infant's pool of primal memories is being loaded with unpleasant sensorimotor data, which will be continually re-experienced and projected into the world throughout life. These are the roots of neurosis. To such a person, life generally feels painful and bad.

As Janov says "the way we love children is by fulfilling their basic needs, even before they become children."[31] And "we cannot develop our brains by ourselves. We need the caregiver's input. His or her love governs our brain. His or her rejection deforms our brain."[32]

THE TOXIC MIND HYPOTHESIS

Continual Repression of Fear Memories Precipitates Neural Toxification

Van Winkle has speculated about the biological dynamics of neurosis.[33] According to her, the nerve cells of the autonomic nervous system are labeled either noradrenergic or cholinergic, depending upon what neurotransmitters they use to project information across synaptic space. The nerve cells of the sympathetic arm of the autonomic nervous system use noradrenaline for this purpose. The parasympathetic arm uses choline.

Stressful experiences in our lives evoke the sympathetic response and the physiological consequences in our body are initiated by a cascade of noradrenergic-facilitated communication between cells in this system.

If primal theory and fear memory research are correct about the primal or fear memory-making process, then the original fear making experience would be encoded on protein molecules along noradrenergic neural circuits. The initial reaction to the fearful situation excites the sympathetic response, then the overwhelming nature of the traumatic event blocks its subsequent expression via the mechanism of dissociation. That is, noradrenaline is released into synaptic spaces in order to prepare the body for a response to a threatening experience, and then this neurotransmitter is not fully utilized in creating this response. This creates a condition of excessive intracellular accumulation of noradrenaline (NA).

This situation requires the uptake of the neurotransmitter by the issuing neuron. Since new neurotransmitters are continually being manufactured and stored in presynaptic vesicles, some of the excessive synaptic neurotransmitter must be absorbed into the nerve cell body itself. This is accomplished by vacuoles, which can move to the cell membrane, open it, engulf the excessive (therefore, toxic) substance, and encapsulate it within the body of the nerve cell. This is a good example of how cells have evolved a means of temporarily adapting themselves to toxic conditions. The cell can actually encapsulate its toxic environment up to a certain limit. This condition can be seen in the postmortem examination of the brain tissue of psychiatric patients.[34]

If primal theory is correct about the continual presentation of the imprint (automatically recalled fear memories), then each time the memory is recalled, the sympathetic response is reinitiated and more noradrenaline is secreted into the synaptic spaces within the noradrenergic circuits of the autonomic nervous system. In other words, the memory of the original, unintegrated, traumatic experience causes the activation of the sympathetic response over and over again. This fits the definition of a chronic condition. *I assume that this process is at work in Solter's description of children using tears and tantrums to heal unresolved issues. This explains why children rage and cry in a seemingly "irrational" way. They are reacting to the imprint of their original, unprocessed fear experience, rather than to present reality.* Hence, neurosis can be seen as being a chronic neurological condition, with the automatically recalled imprint being the cause.

The mechanism of repression, once again, defeats this response, and the neurotransmitter must once again be uptaken and/or encapsulated by the nerve cell vacuoles. Once this process has been initiated, the level of noradrenaline along the nerve circuits builds, incrementally, to a level at which it can no longer be tolerated. When this is sensed, a detoxification crisis is initiated.

This process involves the partial breakdown of the nerve cell membrane and the dumping of excessive accumulations of noradrenaline into intercellular space. This dumping of toxic levels of noradrenaline results in the over excitation of neurons along adjacent nerve circuits. It is estimated that each nerve cell shares synaptic space with two hundred thousand other nerve cells.[35] The consequence of this dumping is the initiation of a generalized sympathetic discharge. We fly into a misdirected rage. We overreact to seemingly neutral events.

> Because of the spatial nature of nerve transmission, messages may travel through alternate neurons causing distorted and compulsive thinking, delusions, hallucinations, psychosis and unintended behavior. As a result of a vicarious elimination of toxins a person might direct rage inwardly as suicidal behavior or toward an innocent person in an aggressive assault.[36]

This discharge is misdirected because the nervous system has displaced the fear memory from conscious thought process and integration. So, when the fear memory is retrieved (remember, only the physical sensations of a fear memory are retrieved), there is no self-awareness involved. There is no directing of thought toward the actual cause of the fear memory. This means that, within the fear memory holding circuit, only enough of a stimulation is initiated to reduce the levels of noradrenaline to a point just beneath which the detoxification crisis can be initiated. Then the process terminates. This leaves a toxic nerve circuit, which is forever hovering just below the limits of detoxification crisis. The neurotic mind is, thus, a toxic mind.

As was stated previously, the successive repression of the sympathetic response, made possible by the fear memory-making and retrieval process and dissociation, results in the accumulation of toxic levels of noradrenaline in neural cell bodies.

It has also been stated that the mind brings up memories as a result of a current trigger, having the same feeling as the memory.

Additionally, it has been speculated that memory is encoded on protein molecules and that these molecules must be broken down and reassembled with each memory recall. A recalled memory, its appearance before the mind's eye, may be the released memory data in its original energy state, after having been freed from the bondage of the protein molecules. As the molecules reassemble, the energy state may be "embodied" in protein, once again, for subsequent storage and retrieval.

Therefore, the triggering of a fear memory by a present situation necessitates the breakdown of the protein memory vehicle. Breakdown byproducts of protein are acidic. And, an acidic nerve environment both contributes to the toxic load and assists the partial breakdown of the neuron and the resultant dumping of excessive toxins. The recollection of a fear memory that is stored along neural circuits that are saturated with toxic levels of noradrenaline initiates the breakdown of parts of the nerve cell and a subsequent detoxification crisis.

Because the fear memory is continually suppressed, the nerve cells on which it is stored never get cleared of toxic metabolites. They are continually hovering at the edge of detoxification crisis—forever awaiting the next trigger. Van Winkle thinks that the act-out (or, behavioral symptom) is the nervous system's way of attempting to trigger this crisis, since the initial part of the crisis is stimulatory. According to her, this is the basis of addiction.

Because of the immediate nature of the fear memory (its lack of occurrence within the domain of self-awareness), it is automatically linked to whatever triggered the recall: that is the fear reaction is mistakenly experienced as having been caused by the trigger. Hence, one always hears in neurotic acting out: "Look what *you* made me do!" "*You* made me angry." "*You're* driving me to drink." *In neurosis there is no awareness that the fear response is being generated internally.* This is because the fear memory is encapsulated in the right hemisphere, uninformed by left-hemisphere logic functions.

Because the noradrenergic neural network on which the primal memory is stored is hovering on the brink of a detoxification crisis, it is continually ready to be discharged by anything that increases the toxic load. That "anything" could be the next fear memory retrieval, which results in the acidic breakdown of the toxic nerve circuit.

In summary, then, something in the present occurs that feels like the original fearful experience. This feeling marker stimulates the toxified primal neural circuit. The protein molecules upon which the memory is stored are broken down. This results in the retrieval of the memory, its projection onto the triggering object, and the generation of acidic metabolic breakdown byproducts (resulting from the protein disassembly). The consequence of the memory retrieval is, thus, a neurotic acting out accompanied by a massive sympathetic discharge.

The discharge is linked to no specific past object because of the dissociative process. Hence, it is projected onto the source of the present trigger. Van Winkle refers to this as a *vicarious detoxification crisis*. This term may be a description of Janov's definition of an abreaction. This will be discussed later.

One can think of the neurotic act-out as an automatic attempt to stimulate a detoxification crisis. But, because the act-out is, by definition, a response that is directed onto the wrong object, the source of the act-out—the memory that is encoded on atrophied noradrenergic nerve circuits—is never fully released (that is, the proper memory holding nerve circuit is never stimulated beyond the threshold of the detoxification crisis).

In other words, we are continually getting angry at whoever or whatever triggers our fear response. But the true source of the original fear memory is blocked from self-awareness by the process of dissociation. If this is true, then the only way to clear the fear memory circuit is to continually direct the thoughts toward the causal agent of the original fear memory. *The left-hemisphere, frontal structure of the brain will automatically accomplish this, if the memory can be presented to it in a way that disables the dissociative process.* This is the goal of primal therapy. And this is why it is a curative rather than palliative therapy.

ARTHUR JANOV'S EVIDENCE

Janov speaks of neurosis as being a lack of communication between the two hemispheres of the brain.[37] The imprint is stored in the right hemisphere and, because of the dissociative function, is isolated from the left hemisphere. The two parts of the brain are unaware of one another. His process of primalling the imprint results in a connection between these hemispheres with regard to the imprint. This connection is the goal of therapy. Because the imprint makes a connection with the left hemisphere, it gets time contextualized. Before the primal, the imprint comes and goes in the present, as is the nature of a conditioned response. After the primal, the imprint comes and goes with the felt sense that the reaction belongs in the past. During the primal process one slowly becomes aware that present experience may not be causing one's current fear reaction. And, if it is not, where else can it be coming from? The response is being generated internally. In other words, there evolves the ability to think logically about current emotional reactions. Logic and time sequencing are functions of the left hemisphere. Because of connection, a rift in the stimulus-response nature of the conditioned fear memory is created. This rift signals the beginning of the healing process. As the primal process continues, the rift widens, and one is presented with more and more of an opportunity to logically examine the triggered emotional response.

It is Janov's contention that this connection is objectively demonstrable via vital sign measurement and by the process of brain mapping.[38] His studies have demonstrated that primal therapy has a normalizing effect on the autonomic nervous system.

His therapists take the patient's vital signs (temperature, blood pressure, and pulse) before and after a session. If connection has occurred in a session, all of the vital signs fall below the baseline (before session) measurements in concert with one another. In Janov's view, if the measurements are erratic and do not fall below baseline measurements, the patient has only abreacted.

Another objective test of connection is brain wave activity before and after the therapy. Janov also considers EEG responses a vital sign measurement. Studies done at four major universities have shown how reliving pain changes the brain map. In general, the EEG studies

> reveal changes in brainwave frequency and amplitude after the patient gains access to and resolves traumatic memory. They indicate that the brainwave patterns of advanced primal patients are less repressed and less busy. The brainwaves are better synchronized and slower, and the amplitudes are more evenly distributed over the whole brain. We also see a better balance of activity between the right and left hemispheres.[39]

Additionally, with the advent of new software, real time studies of patients' brainwave activity during a session is now possible. Janov claims that by the study of the patient's delta, theta, alpha, and beta wave activity, it is now possible to study the patient's progress in a session. The type of brain-wave activity at any particular time tells the therapist at which level of consciousness the client is processing information.

These studies have been reported in the *UCLA Brain Research Bulletin* and *Acta Scandinavia*. Yet, even though conventional psychotherapy has demanded "objectively verifiably data" none of these studies are referenced in the literature.

Finally, the spontaneous welling up of insights after a session is a subjective, but very important, indication that connection has occurred. According to Janov, the client's surety that the insight is real is "a second major indication of a true primal experience."[40]

My experimental data supports Janov's assertion that primal facilitation has a normalizing influence on the stress adaptation response of the autonomic nervous system. A summary of this data is presented in the Appendix.

THE MIND'S EYE

Any study of primal facilitation should include an awareness of how one attends to what is being relived. It is generally understood that to recall information is to hold a visual image up before the mind's eye. And, whenever this is done, there is the sense that the object of consideration belongs in the past. That is, the data from the recalled memory is time-contextualized.

During a recollection, the mental image exists, three-dimensionally, in the mind, and it is also being observed. The ability to observe mental images is referred to as the "mind's eye." It is one aspect of evolving self-awareness. Yet, science does not understand this function at all. The study of self-awareness is at the cutting edge of neuroscience. And, it is critically important to understanding the process of primal therapy.

Damasio reminds the reader that mental images are not just visual. "By the term images I mean mental patterns with a structure built with the tokens of each of the sensory modalities—visual, auditory, olfactory, gustatory, and somatosensory."[41] For instance: how is one aware that one is in a certain body position, when one cannot see oneself in this position. The answer is that sensorimotor data from many proprioceptors throughout the body is being presented to image space. When the question of position is posed, this implicit data is drawn into image space, where the mind's eye is able to reflect upon the nonvisual image being created by this data. And, the answer is thereby known. In other words, a visual image of oneself lying down is not necessary to knowing that one's position is such and such. The mind has assembled a sensorimotor image in this case. And this image is reflected upon by the mind's eye in the same way as is a visual image. This reflection results in knowing about our present position in space. The construction of an image takes place "when we engage objects, from persons and places to toothaches, from the outside of the brain toward its inside; or when we reconstruct objects from memory, from the inside out, as it were."[42]

All of our memories, the record of every one of our experiences, "exists in dispositional form (a synonym for *implicit, covert, nonconscious*), waiting to become an explicit image or action."[43]

Finally, Damasio says that the "*image space* is that in which images of all sensory types occur explicitly."[44] This image space may be Damasio's way of describing the window or energy field in which sensory data is gathered and held up for consideration by the "mind's eye."

When an implicit memory is recalled, it is done automatically (it does not require conscious effort). Two types of implicit memory are: procedural (memory for skills, which become automatic over time) and dispositional (behaviors learned through classical or operant conditioning). In order to ride a bike or to react in fear to something, one does not have to consciously recall the memory. It is automatically retrieved. And, we do not reflect upon these memories. They are not held up to the mind's eye.

Fear memories are dispositional memories.

Damasio states that we make dispositional memories explicit by bringing them into the image space.

With regard to dissociated dispositional memories (fear memories), however, a little more is required. Attention must be paid to sensory overload. This is because the brain automatically reacts to sensory overload by dissociating it away from image space. So, this automatic defensive function must be overcome in order to bring fear memory into image space. Janov refers to this as working within a "sensory window."

Also, since dispositional memories happen to us, one cannot consciously direct their emergence as one does normal declarative memories. Rather, one sets the stage on which these memories are automatically triggered.

HOMEOPATHY
THE NATURE OF SYMPTOMS

Samuel Hahnemann was a German physician and chemist who left the orthodox medical profession because he felt that the accepted "state of the art" medical practices of his day, such as bloodletting, poisonous doses of mercury and arsenic, and other treatments of disease were harmful. His discovery that substances in small doses stimulate the organism to heal that which they cause in overdose led him to formulate the Law of Similars, which is the basic principle of homeopathy.

> Hahnemann's observation that a substance able to mimic a sick person's symptoms can help cure the patient prompted a revolutionary understanding of symptoms. Instead of assuming that symptoms represent illogical, improper, or unhealthy responses of the body and that they should be treated, controlled, and suppressed, Hahnemann learned that symptoms are positive adaptive responses to the variety of stresses the body experiences. Symptoms represent the body's best effort to heal itself. Hence, instead of suppressing symptoms, therapies should stimulate the body's defenses to complete the curative process.[45]

Hahnemann also believed that "a person's inherent healing powers were so strong that only a small stimulus is needed to begin the healing process." And "once the healing process begins, it is best to do nothing more but let the process continue in its own way."[46]

A common experience of those who use homeopathic medicines to treat chronic conditions is that symptoms may initially get worse in the process of a cure. This is sometimes referred to as the "aggravation" of symptoms.

Likewise, during primal facilitation, behavioral aggravation of symptoms may occur because facilitation is stimulating the atrophied neural circuits upon which the fear memories are stored. Because the circuits are being reenergized, they become better able to release the fear memory. This increased ability appears as an aggravation. That is, the behavioral symptoms may initially get worse in the healing process.

A facilitator of naturopathic emotional healing, likewise, sees symptoms (neurotic behavior, in the case of emotional disorder) as the body's continual attempt to get rid of the underlying cause of the problem. This means that the act-out is the attempt of the person to initiate a detoxification crisis. The problem is that the act out is directed onto the wrong object.

Because of the disconnect between the encapsulated primal memory and left-brain logic functions, we believe that our present triggered fear reaction is being caused by what is happening right now.

The process of primal therapy can be seen as an attempt to exacerbate the various symptoms of neurosis by paying attention to the rising pain of the primal memory. This memory is full of fear, misery, and tears. To feel the content of this memory, to experience the pain in small doses and to rage about it (in its original context), is to initiate the healing process. An "overdose" of painful information is what triggered the dissociative process. This process, in turn, set up the conditions for the development of the chronic condition of neurosis. A reexperiencing of this painful information "in small doses" stimulates a "healing crisis." These healing crises begin to reverse the chronic neurotic condition. As Janov says, primal therapy is neurosis in reverse. Thus, the primal facilitation process embodies the homeopathic belief that "like cures like." Afterward, the crying and tears is the healing phase or recovery period of the crisis.

Within each emotional healing session, then, the facilitator helps the client to experience "in small doses" that which caused the neurosis "in overdose."

The phrase "in small doses" implicitly embodies the importance of Janov's sensory window concept in therapy.

This action thereby stimulates the client's natural healing process. Thus, the primal oriented, naturopathic, emotional healing process can be seen as being a homeopathic activity.

Chapter 2
Endnotes

1. A. Young, *The Secret Afterlife of Freud's Traumatic Neurosis*, Abstract, (Vortrag auf der AG-Sitzung am, 2002).

2. A. Janov, *The New Primal Scream: Primal Therapy 20 Years On* (Wilmington, DE: Enterprise Publishing, 1991), 105.

3. Janov, *The New Primal Scream*, 33.

4. D. P. Henderson, *Panacea: A New Non-Medical Approach to Mental Health and Emotional Control* (Fawnskin, CA: Scientific Specialists, 1995).

5. (2003, August). Available: http://www2.wcoil.com/~awards/memory.htm

6. J. LeDoux (2005, February). LeDoux Laboratory.
   Available: http://www.cns.nyu.edu/home/ledoux/overview.htm

7. A. Janov, *Why You get Sick. How You Get Well: The Healing Power of Feelings* (West Hollywood, CA: Dove Books, 1996), 42-3.

8. Janov, *Why You Get Sick*, 190.

9. B. H. Lipton, (2005, February), *The New Biology. Available: http://www. brucelipton.com/print.php*

10. B. A. van der Kolk, A. C. McFarlane, and L. Weisaeth, *Traumatic Stress. The Effects of Overwhelming Experience on Mind, Body and Society* (New York: The Guilford Press, 1996).

11. LeDoux, memories fixed by intensity of feeling.

12. LeDoux, *Nature* 406, (2000): 722-6.

13. B. A. van der Kolk and R. Fisler (2002, June), *Dissociation and the Fragmentary Nature of Traumatic Memories: Overview and Exploratory Study*. Available: http://www.trauma-pages.com/vanderk2.htm, 8.

14. B. A. van der Kolk, (2002, June, P3), *SCORE: Memory and the Evolving Psychobiology of Post Traumatic Stress*: Available: http://www.trauma-pages.com/vanderk4.htm

15. A. Janov, *Why You Get Sick. How You get Well. The Healing Power of Feelings* (West Hollywood, CA: Dove Books, 1996), 209.

16. B. A. van der Kolk (2002, June), Trauma Information Pages, *In Terror's Grip: Healing the Ravages of Trauma*. Available: http://www.trauma-pages.com, 4.

17. Ibid., 4.

18. Ibid., 4.

19. Ibid., 6.

20. Ibid., 7.

21. J. LeDoux (2002, July) LeDoux Laboratory, *Overview. Emotion, Memory, and the Brain: What the Lab Does and Why We Do It.* http://www/cns.nyuedu/hoe.ledoux/overview.htm

22. A. Janov and E. M. Holden, *Primal Man: The New Consciousness* (New York: Thomas Y. Crowell Company, 1975), 5.

23. B. A. van der Kolk and R. Fisler (2002, June), *Dissociation and the Fragmentary Nature of Traumatic Memories: Overview and Exploratory Study.* Available: http://www.trauma-pages.com/vanderk2.htm, 6.

24. S. M. Baker, *Detoxification and Healing: The Key to Optimal Health* (New Canaan, CT: Keats Publishing, Inc., 1997), 173.

25. W. H. Frey II, *Crying: The Mystery of Tears* (Minneapolis, MN: Winston Press, Inc., 1985).

26. A. Solter, *Tears and Tantrums: What to Do When Babies and Children Cry*, 2nd ed. (Goleta, CA: Shining Star Press, 1998), 5.

27. S. M. Baker, *Detoxification and Healing: The Key to Optimal Health* (New Canaan, CT: Keats Publishing, Inc., 1997), 141.

28. M. Henningsen, (2005, February), *Attachment Disorder: Theory, Parenting, and Therapy.* Available: http://www.netaxs.com/~sparky/adoption/attach_3.htm

29. A. Schore, *Affect Dysregulation and Disorders of the Self* (New York: 2003).

30. M. Henningsen, (2005, February), *Attachment Disorder: Theory, Parenting, and Therapy.* Available: http://www.netaxs.com/~sparky/adoption/attach_3.htm

31. A. Janov, *The Biology of Love* (Amherst, NY: Prometheus Books, 2000), 263.

32. Janov, *The Biology of Love,* 221.

33. E. Van Winkle, "The Toxic Mind: the Biology of Mental Illness and Violence." *Medical Hypothesis* 55(4), 2000: 356-68.

34. Ibid., 363.

35. Ibid., 361.

36. Ibid., 361.

37. A. Janov, *Why You Get Sick: How You Get Well* (West Hollywood, CA: Dove Books, 1996), 207.

38. Janov, *Why You Get Sick,* 255.

39. Ibid., 255-56.

40. Ibid., 231.

41. A. Damasio, *The Feeling of What Happens: Body and Emotion in the Making of Consciousness* (New York: Harcourt Brace and Company, 1999), 318.

42. Ibid., 318-17.

43. Ibid., 332.

44. Ibid., 331.

45. S. Cummings and D. Ullman, *Everybody's Guide to Homeopathic Medicines,* 3rd rev ed. (New York: Jeremy P. Tarcher/Putnam, 1997), 5.

46. S. Cummings, et al., *Everybody's Guide to Homeopathic Medicines,* 9.

3

Implications

A NATUROPATHIC ANATOMY OF NEUROSIS

Conventional allopathic psychotherapy is not concerned with the ultimate causes of emotional disorders. Indeed, it seems to pride itself in the atheoretical model to which it has been forced by the lack of an adequate causal explanation. On the other hand, Janov has presented the field with an explanatory causal hypothesis and has demonstrated that his hypothesis has objectively verifiable and repeatable predictive power. Because of this, he has referred to primal therapy as the first scientific psychotherapy. And because his hypothesis addresses causes, it can be considered a naturopathic modality.

By synthesizing Henderson's memory theory, Solter's theory of child development and Janov's imprint hypothesis, I have constructed a reasonable naturopathic theory about the development of neurosis.[1]

Within the womb, a non-nurturing, stressful environment results in the creation of a pool of distressing sensorimotor memories. This, in turn, creates a condition in which the newborn can spontaneously and chronically re-experience this distressing sensorimotor data. This may be the reason why some newborns are considered "colic" or problematic.

Whenever the infant experiences a truly distressing stimulus, it responds by getting angry and crying. Its parents then know that something is wrong and respond by taking away the distressing stimulus. This might be hunger, a wet diaper, etc. The child might cry for a while afterward, but then its balance is restored. Or, it may be startled by something in its environment and turn to its mother for help in processing this disturbing event.

If its parents do not respond properly to its needs, the pain of deprivation increases. But the pain cannot increase indefinitely, or it would die. There is a level at which the nervous system begins to block the pain signals. This is a survival mechanism and is the substrate of the dissociative process.

Once this level is reached, the frightening experience loses its "window of opportunity" to be processed, the sympathetic response is truncated, and a fear memory of the distressing stimulus is created, along with a neurotic tension in the body. That is, something distressing has happened to the body that it has been unable to process (because of poor attention by the caregiver), so it files the event away for future reference (in the form of uncomfortable body sensations).

I would like to define tension as a force that is generated in any natural system that becomes unbalanced (i.e., water trapped behind a dam). Once a dam is constructed in a waterway, constricting the normal flow of water, the water behind the dam is forever generating a force on the walls of the dam, trying to get back to its normal, level flow. This force is called potential energy and it increases in direct proportion to the amount of obstruction.

Neurotic tension (emotional potential energy) is nature's way of creating the possibility of reestablishing emotional balance (resolution) in a disturbed emotional process. With the establishment of chronic fear memory retrieval, nature presents an opportunity to offer up the original fear memory to a healing window of opportunity over and over again.

Because of the automatic retrieval function, these memories keep resurfacing and stimulating sympathetic responses. This is fear memory retrieval.

The retrieval of the fear memory results in a response to a real physical stimulus: a heightening of the autonomic sympathetic response system. With the memory release, one begins to reexpress the sensorimotor/emotional discomfort of the original (unresolved) traumatic incident.

What is different in this situation is that no present need is triggering this activation. Rather, a memory is triggering it: something from the past.

So, now there exists a situation in which a real, present sympathetic response is occurring because of a past memory intrusion. This past memory intrusion is not visible, and it is not a response to a present condition. So, the child's behavior is seen as being functionally disordered since there is no apparent physical cause. This is the definition of neurosis.

Thus, the child's spontaneous attempt to heal itself from a past trauma by raging and crying in the present can be seen as rudimentary neurotic behavior. The neurotic process started because the trauma went unprocessed when it originally occurred.

Now, the child's behavior seems irrational to the parents. They want it to stop. So, they begin to teach the child control patterns. They teach it how to distract itself from its discomfort. These can be pleasurable such as giving sweets and food, even though the child is not hungry and painful such as threatening abandonment and shaming behavior. The child soon learns that certain substances can buffer its angry and tearful feelings. It learns that something bad will happen when it cries or gets angry. It learns to respond to fear memory intrusions in ways that blunt the physical effects of the intrusions while, simultaneously, gaining the parent's approval. It gets this approval and feels better, even though the fear memories continue to exist and will continue to exert their effects. And when they come up again, the child acts out again, instead of responding appropriately to the signals of the fear memory. That is, one learns how to continually call upon one's learned proxy tools of repression to dull the constantly emerging fear sensations.

A situation has now been set up in the child's nervous system in which there is a functional disconnect between a very real stimulus (fear memory content) and a healing response to that stimulus: anger and crying. The fear memory content is always coming up and is never allowed to be expressed. The child learns how to do this automatically. And the nerve circuits on which this content is stored gradually atrophy and become increasingly toxified with excessive, unexpressed noradrenaline.

With maturity comes the acquisition of more and more complex ways in which to be distracted from this fear memory content. The most impressive distraction comes from the maturation of the highest brain structure. One learns that words and ideas can be used to defend against uncomfortable feelings. One of the functions of the frontal cortex is to modulate conditioned fear responses. The adult cortex is so powerful that one can use it to block lower-level pain signals. Evidence of this is quite dramatic during hypnosis when someone fails to feel a pin prick, upon receiving the suggestion that the pin is a feather. Some forms of meditation do this. One can quite powerfully use meditation to quiet a busy mind and to lower core body functions and stress. But too many people pay too little attention to why the chronic stress is there in the first place. Chronic stress is symptomatic of a deeper process (constant fear memory retrieval). Hence, meditation is blocking the pain signals temporarily. Janov's brain scan research has proven that some forms of meditation are pain blockers. And, when engaging in any other activity whose purpose it is to address symptoms, if one discontinues meditation, the fear memory content begins to rise into consciousness once again. This is why everything people do to treat symptoms only they must do habitually and forever. People are forever trimming the leaves from the weed, and they are forever growing back, sometimes more vigorous than before.

The Naturopathic Facilitation of Emotional Wellness
General Considerations

In his online journal, Turton quotes a research paper published in *The New England Journal of Medicine*:

> Extrapolation to the US population suggests that in 1990 Americans made [an] estimated 425 million visits to providers of unconventional therapy. This number exceeds the number of visits to all US primary care physicians (388 million). Expenditures associated with use of unconventional therapy in 1990 amounted to approximately $13.7 billion, three quarters of which ($10.3 billion) was paid out of pocket. This figure is comparable to the $12.8 billion spent out of pocket annually for all hospitalizations in the United States.[2]

Judging by the dollars that Americans are spending on alternative medical treatments, there is an emerging awareness in our country that conventional medical treatment (the treatment of symptoms) is not enough. There is a strong call to join naturopathic healing modalities with the conventional treatment of disease. The online medical resource, National Library of Medicine (NLM), now contains an entire section of references to naturopathic research papers. This branch is called Complimentary and Alternative Medicine (CAM). It is time to consider a naturopathic psychotherapy. It is time to consider a therapy that claims to heal emotional problems rather than just treating the symptoms.

In naturopathic medicine the foundational assumption is that cellular toxicosis is the underlying condition of disease. This condition generates the multiple symptoms, which traditionally are associated with separate diseases. However, there is only one disease: toxicosis. Treat the toxic state, not the symptoms of that state.

So, instead of generating a catalog of symptoms, each group of which are treated as distinct "disease entities," a naturopathic emotional healing modality would proceed on the assumption that one underlying condition generates the multiple abnormal behaviors that we refer to as neurosis. That underlying condition is the existence of amygdalic memories of traumatic events: primal memories, fear memories, or Janov's imprints. Their chronic activation and repression precipitates cellular toxicity in the neural circuits on which the fear memories are encoded. The physiological consequences of this toxicosis produce periodic over and under excitation of the nervous system. Logically then, if facilitation can remove the one underlying condition, neural toxicity and unwanted behavioral symptoms should disappear.

In this way one can see that the ordering of abnormal behavior in primal therapy, and its subsequent treatment, is naturopathic. The task of any natural emotional healing process, then, is to eliminate the toxic condition. The source of the toxic condition is eliminated when the primal memory is integrated into the whole psychic structure. Successful integration of a painful primal memory removes the chronic condition, whereby nerve circuits are toxified. Resolution can now be defined as the termination of a detoxification process.

Janov has been consistently adamant in his refusal to teach the techniques of primal therapy to anyone other than his students. In addition to this, his therapy is extremely expensive and requires traveling and paying for room-and-board in the Los Angeles area, which is in itself a large expense. The reality is that very few people can afford his therapy. And, most insurance plans today will only pay for limited conventional "talk style therapies" and unlimited treatment with psychotropic medication. Furthermore, each provider claim must be keyed into one of the DMV-generated "illness" categories.

So, a naturopathic emotional wellness therapy exists that, unlike other naturopathic therapies, has no means of reaching the people on an affordable, grassroots level. How then can this therapy ever reach the masses of people in need of relief from neurotic suffering?

While he does not go into the specifics of the therapeutic process, Janov does present in his books some very important general guidelines for correct therapy. And, if I am correct in my conclusion that all neuroses are post-traumatic stress disorders, then guidelines for effective facilitation can be developed from Janov's general ideas, as well as by studying the information that is presented in this book.

Previously, I had concluded that spontaneous crying and raging in children (when this behavior is not the result of immediate need or want) is neurotic behavior in its simplest form. It is neurotic in the sense that Janov has discussed. That is: the feeling is correct, but the context is wrong. The child is crying and raging in the present about a stressor that occurred in the past. This phenomenon is made possible by the formation of imprints or painful primal memories and their constant intrusion into the present situation. This is the neurobiological mechanism that Janov was looking for that would explain how a trauma in one's past could emerge in the present. Adult neurotic behavior is not different from this basic infant response. It is just more complex. The adult has learned to use complicated behaviors as compensating mechanisms for not having been allowed to respond naturally to traumatic experiences.

A naturopathic facilitator must support the client's retrieval and integration of fearful primal memories. The moderated feeling and integration of fear memories seems to act in much the same way as the "delete message" command acts on a computer. That is, a file is deleted by taking away its name tag. And, although the content of that file still exists within the memory system of the computer, it can no longer be retrieved.

Likewise, the primal memory integration process seems to take away the primal memory's feeling tag. "Feeling the feeling" removes the feeling tag. If the feeling tag is removed, a primal memory can no longer be automatically retrieved by present-day triggers. If it can no longer be retrieved, its physiological content can no longer be re-experienced by the body. If it can no longer be re-experienced by the body, it is no longer being reacted to. As a consequence, the client can no longer "act out" neurotically.

> The resolution of a neurotic act-out is not dependent upon a consciously directed, rational thought process. Rather, it is the automatic consequence of having re-experienced and integrated a previously isolated and unintegrated fear memory. This is the central philosophical difference between primal therapy and conventional behavioral-oriented psychotherapy.

By its very nature, the process of natural emotional healing must be gradual. One must remember that the individual initially created and stored fear memories because he experienced them as overwhelming and uncontrollable in the original instance. And, most importantly, these memories are multi-leveled, having a conceptual, emotional, and sensorimotor component. The process of primal therapy is the feeling (deleting) of three-leveled portions of each of these memories. This process starts with the least fearful primal memories and proceeds down the "chain of pain" to the most fearful of the primal memories. As one follows the chain, the body's resistance to feeling the feeling increases. The "charge" of the pain increases as earlier and earlier painful primal memories are accessed. This is because the younger one was when these painful feelings were experienced, the less control one had over the events. Unmet needs are a life and death experience for infants. The body reacted accordingly.

Therefore, the environment in which the feelings are felt must be completely supportive. This therapy must be attended to by someone who has participated in his own primal therapy or by the rare person who was raised according to parenting principles like those expounded by Aletha Soltier. This experience teaches the facilitator that there is nothing to fear about expressing anger. There is, likewise, no shame involved in crying as deeply as needed. A facilitator who has not felt and expressed his own anger and shame feelings will automatically get uncomfortable around people who begin to express these emotions. It is an autonomic response and is out of the facilitator's control. Conventional psychotherapeutic practice is mistaken, regarding this issue. It teaches that a therapist can prevent counter-transference onto the client by "understanding" how it occurs and being ready for it. A triggered sympathetic response cannot be "understood" away. Rather, when a therapist begins to get triggered, he will unconsciously attempt to remove himself from this uncomfortable feeling by maneuvering the client away from her feelings, perhaps by getting her to talk about them rather than raging or crying about them. This is precisely what a parent does with a child who is acting out in an unexplainable way. Thus, a triggered therapist may repeat the mistake of the attachment disordered parent. The feeling of one's feeling may be so scary that the situation may require physical contact for the client, since human contact is our earliest and most powerful means of feeling loved and supported. Conventional psychotherapy has curtailed physical contact with the client, thereby removing one of the most powerful and biologically fundamental means of helping someone feel safe and cared for. Little by little, if the environment is safe, the client feels and integrates the fear memory content, thereby making it inaccessible to further retrieval. Little by little, the act out becomes less and less compelling.

The rate at which primal memories are released is critical to the emotional healing process. Stone postulates the existence of a brain "governor" that is active in fear memory processing.[3] He compares the reservoir of fear memories to water trapped behind a stick dam. The water is higher in back of the dam than it is in front of the dam. This gives the trapped memories a strong potential for generating power when the memories are released. One could equate the degree of potential energy of the stored water with the degree of neurotic tension that the client experiences in his life. The more "water behind the dam," the more neurotic tension present in the client.

Stone's idea is naturopathic. He believes that this governor is there to protect the psychic structure of the mind by only releasing as much of the memory as can be integrated at any one time. It is logical to assume that, if there is a natural function that automatically reacts to protect us from the disruption of self-awareness (during the original event), it would react in the same way to protect us from the reemerging memory of the original event, if it is once again presented in a way that is overwhelming to conscious awareness. In other words, *dissociation is triggered by real, immediate experience as well as by the memory of this experience.*

To assume the truth of the naturopathic belief that the body can govern fear memory formation and its release is, again, to trust nature's wisdom regarding self-healing. Janov's primal therapy becomes decidedly un-naturopathic on this point. It is his belief that human beings do not have the inherent ability to coherently release their imprints: therefore, the process must be directed by the therapist. In fact, he likens the primal process to effecting brain surgery. And, by analogy, only brain surgeons should do it. By this he means his own students. I agree with Janov's concern, but only in the case of severe orbitofrontal pruning due to severe early abuse and in cases of later trauma that are so severe that the client is unable to function in society. In the former case, the client lacks the brain structure necessary to modulate the fear memory retrieval process. In the latter case, the sensory data of the traumatic experience outstrips the brain's ability to modulate its effects. These clients may become easily overwhelmed by and re-traumatized by the therapeutic process. So, a more structured form of therapy is needed. Based upon my own experiences in therapy, as well as my experiences in working with clients, I believe that, in all other cases, the client possesses the innate ability to modulate and process fear memory data, as long as this process is not forced. This means that the majority of the human population can be safely facilitated by lay people who have undergone their own facilitation and who have had training in primal facilitation. This, in turn, means that this emotional wellness process can reach the people in much the same way as massage and other naturopathic modalities are reaching people.

Stone's dam analogy speaks to the importance of a controlled release of fear memories.

This was the mistake that early primal therapists made. They believed that a client's defenses should be "busted." To use Stone's analogy, they believed that the dam should be torn down in large chunks, rather than stick by stick. In this way, neurosis could be cured quickly. This was an overly optimistic idea that failed because it did not take into account the brain's need to protect the integrity or continuity of its self-awareness function.

If one continues with Stone's analogy, one can understand the importance of a slow, controlled release of trapped fear memories. Just as the total destruction of a dam would release huge amounts of water capable of eroding all that is below that dam, a "busting" of the client's defenses, which lie in front of his reservoir of fear memories, would release large amounts of energy capable of disintegrating the client's self-awareness. Again, one must remember that an overwhelming flood of painful experience is what the nervous system was protecting self-aware-ness against originally. It is why the fear memory was created in the first place. So, it is important that the therapeutic experience not duplicate the traumatic condi-tion in which the fear memory was originally formed. This is referred to as re-traumatization.

Rather, a naturopathic facilitator understands the intelligence and safety inherent in the client's removal of the dam stick by stick. When sitting with a cli-ent, the facilitator sees that the release of fear memories has a cycle. The anger and fear that is brought up has a beginning and an end. So does the crying. This cycle occurs spontaneously (if the client feels that it is safe to do so) and the pro-cess is controlled entirely by the client.

When one or two sticks are removed and the process cycles down, the poten-tial energy of the water behind the dam is lowered slightly and at a rate that can be integrated. And the water that is released flows into a balanced state with the water that is below the dam. Put another way, because there was a slow and con-trolled release, the environment below the dam has a chance to absorb the water release without creating damage to that environment. Just as the newly released water is absorbed into the soil below the dam, a newly felt primal memory is absorbed safely into the entire psychic structure. The fear memory is now con-nected to both hemispheres of the brain. It now has access to left-hemisphere logic functions. It is no longer a right-hemisphere encapsulation.

The homeostatic adjustment that was described above is termed resolution or integration. And it is a whole body/brain readjustment or balancing. It leads automatically to a decrease of neurotic tension, which is directly proportional to the extent of the memory retrieval and integration and is objectively verifiable in the permanent normalization of vital sign activity and brain function.

PROVOKING THE HEALING CRISIS

> It is not the trauma itself that is the source of illness but the uncon-scious, repressed, hopeless despair over not being allowed to give expres-sion to what one has suffered.—Alice Miller[4]

To understand the process of primal therapy one must first understand how the nervous system processes experience. "It is the limbic system, particularly the hippocampus and amygdala with their direct connections to the frontal cortex, which acts as a 'gate to consciousness'"[5] Experience is processed, initially, through the early, feeling brain, which has been referred to as the limbic system. This is why memories are coded by feeling markers, rather than names (we were feeling beings long before we had language). This system assesses the emotional content of the experience and, in turn, feeds the information down to the reticular activating system (RAS), a part of the brainstem, and upward to the frontal cortex.

In a nonthreatening situation, the information is encoded within the hippocampal memory system as a declarative memory. Implicit in this event is the presentation of the experience to image space and, thus, consideration by the mind's eye. The stimulus that the RAS receives activates the HPA axis and the forebrain, which orchestrates physical responses to the experience. Within the left hemisphere of the frontal cortex, this new information is collated with the totality of experience, and rational responses are initiated. Because we processed the experience in the left frontal cortex, the experience is understood holistically, as one event among many in our lives. The experience is remembered within a time matrix. We can, thereafter, tell a story about this experience, thereby integrating it into our lives. And, whenever we recall the event, it will carry with it a sense of having happened in the past.

In a fear-related situation, one in which there is high stress and a feeling of having no control over the outcome, the stress hormone cortisol interferes with the hippocampal memory formation process, as well as the integrative activity of the frontal cortex. As a result of this interference, declarative memory is not encoded or, to the extent that it is, the memory is fragmented. Excessive cortisol also interferes with the frontal cortex functions of organization of experience and proper response.

"When people are frightened or aroused the frontal areas of the brain, which analyze an experience and associate it with other knowledge, are deactivated."[6] In other words, the brain senses this overwhelming information as being disruptive to our higher consciousness—our "sense of self." Since it is a function of the brain to remember experience, particularly fear-related experience, the experience is shunted to, and encoded within, the primitive amygdalic memory system. This memory contains only the (sensorimotor) feelings and emotions that one had during the experience. This process effectively encapsulates the fear-related memory within the right hemisphere of the brain. Since the overwhelming experience was not properly processed by the left frontal cortex, it was never integrated as "part of our personal story." The event was not integrated into the entire psychic structure.

Since it is also the function of the brain to bring up memory as a way of informing present felt experience, these fear-related memories are always restimulating the RAS, which stimulates the HPA axis and the frontal cortex of the brain. As a result, vital functions are always being disturbed and the mind is always "racing" when the reality of the present moment seems not to warrant this reaction. This is what may be occurring in the child who starts raging and crying for "no apparent reason." In an adult, this process might result in a scenario in which one is walking down the street and "for no reason" becomes aware of carrying on an angry argument with oneself. The blood pressure is up. The fists and jaw are clenched. The heart is beating rapidly. Yet nothing in the present is causing this (very real) reaction. This example describes the recall of a fearful amygdalic memory. And, because it was originally encapsulated from the frontal integration functions, one cannot sense that it is something that happened in the past. It feels like "now."

So, in reaction to uncontrollable fear, the brain sets up a closed loop of information processing—a "mindless" stimulus response situation: a conditioned fear response. Thereafter, any experience in the present, which has the feeling of an existing fear-related primal memory, has the subsequent fear response projected onto it. That is, the mind automatically associates and generalizes the original experience. And, just as a parent cannot understand the "irrational" raging and crying of an infant, those who are around an adult who is acting out neurotically cannot understand that "irrational" behavior, either. They are the object of a conditioned fear response, just because what is being said or done in that person's presence "feels" like the original source of the fear reaction.

It is in this sense that neurosis can be seen as a "disruption of balance between a person and his environment." Once the conditioned fear response (and its subsequent act-out) is extinguished, one senses that the response was wrong or overly dramatic, or that it felt childish, etc. But there is still no connection made within the left frontal cortex, so it cannot be understood within a time context. It will, therefore, occur over and over again, whenever that fear memory is ignited. One sees this process at work in abusive relationships in which rage is repeatedly directed toward one's mate, followed by feelings of remorse and the unending promises that the rage will never again be repeated.

> Because the frontal cortex (...) is heavily connected to the limbic system, a good fronto-limbic connection can stop the reticular activation.

> That is, when a below-conscious feeling keeps us stirred up, the only
> way to stop that activation permanently is to make a proper connection
> to the subconscious feeling.[7]

And, "It is only when feelings rise to be made frontally conscious that we can say that there is true control."[8]

"Frontal consciousness" of fear memories is the objective of a naturopathic emotional healing process. And it begins with the kindling of a fear memory.

During facilitation, if there is conversation, it is useful only if it segues into a feeling. If role playing or other modes of experiential therapy are used, it is only useful if it segues into a feeling. The ignition of a fear memory, allowing oneself to feel (or re-experience) the feeling, is the goal.

Once the client is in the feeling, the process is self-activating, is self-limiting, and proceeds at its own pace. The facilitator should not interfere with this natural progression, except in ways that help the client to enrich and deepen the feeling, while keeping its expression from escalating out of the sensory window (dissociation).

In fear memory work it is important not to re-traumatize the client. This can happen if the client is overwhelmed with the content of the fear memory (just as was the case in the original, memory-generating event. And it can happen if there is no sense of safety within the therapeutic environment (just as there was no sense of safety during the original event). The safest way to do this work is to feel or experience pieces of the memory on all three levels of consciousness within a safe and supportive environment. And, this modulated reexperiencing is usually all that the "governor" will allow to happen.

In the aftermath of the feeling cycle there is usually a quiet period during which the client begins to integrate the feeling. Whenever a piece of traumatic memory is felt and processed, the client invariably begins to tell a story about this fragment. That is, the client is beginning to integrate this (previously encapsulated) event into a personal story. This means that the (previously encapsulated) feeling made a connection to the left frontal cortex and now can be woven into the fabric of the client's larger, declarative life story. If the facilitator sits quietly with the client during this time (instead of talking or explaining) the client will say something like: "I was just thinking about a time when...," "It's funny, but I just had a memory about how nice my grandfather was to me...," or "I was always by myself...," etc. It is usually easy to see how these statements are connected to what the client was feeling during the session. The client is associating the newly felt memory with others that have the same general feeling.

At this time the facilitator should be careful not to make the connection for the client—no matter how tempting that might be. The therapeutic experience is much more powerful if the client makes the connection. With that connection, the client is beginning to tell a story about a felt piece of a (previously) isolated fear memory. The client is beginning to understand how that piece fits into his life. The felt piece of memory is experienced within a time matrix. With this connection, the process of healing a neurosis has begun.

Note here that the facilitator does not have to explain to the client how that piece fits. This automatic "knowing" is a deeply personal and automatic occurrence. *The mind is deeply integrative once the dissociative process is defeated.*

According to Aletha Solter, "The healing processes of crying and raging are noisy, messy, unpredictable, and time-consuming. They require commitment and attention from caring adults. People are often afraid of strong and painful emotions, and don't know how to deal with them other than to repress them."[9]

Solter is talking about children and their parents. But the process she is describing is also occurring between the client and facilitator within the therapeutic environment.

Caretakers teach children how to repress crying and raging in some of the following ways:[10]

- Telling child to stop crying

- Punishing (or threatening)

- Withdrawing love or attention, isolating child

- Distracting with talk, music, movement, games

- Putting something in child's mouth (food, pacifier)

- Teasing, shaming

- Denying or minimizing child's pain

- Praising child for not crying

- Getting child to talk or laugh

Adults, thus respond to the "inappropriate" tears and tantrums by teaching their children, through fear, shame, or distraction, ways in which to repress this natural healing mechanism. Children learn these lessons well and begin to apply them in their adult emotional lives. This complex of learned repressive techniques becomes nothing more than a complicated, ritualized way of avoiding tears and tantrums.

In this way, the neurotic process was continued by the learning of a devious, obliquely directed way in which to express fear, anger, and sadness. The multitude of ways in which individuals express this cluster of learned repressive techniques is what conventional psychotherapy studies in its attempt to diagnose and categorize mental disorder. Therefore, conventional psychotherapy is studying the varied consequences of repressive techniques, rather than studying the process that the repressive techniques are called upon to mitigate.

If act-outs (behavioral symptoms) are a consequence of the multifaceted suppression of the natural impulse to cry and rage about our unresolved traumatic experiences, then would it not be true that helping an adult to cry and rage about traumatic experiences would eliminate the need to use these "proxy" tools? It is my belief that naturopathic emotional healing is as simple and as difficult as this. It is simple because nature has already evolved the means for recovering from traumatic experience: spontaneous raging and crying. Human beings are born with this natural ability. And, during childhood and throughout adult life, the body is constantly trying to initiate this natural healing cycle.

It is difficult because one is continually struggling to prevent the emergence of this healing cycle because of repressive childhood education. That is, caretaker conditioning has succeeded in unbalancing the natural healing mechanism. And it has done so with distraction, fear, and shaming, which are sociologically powerful and very difficult to overcome. Quite simply, one has been taught that, if one does something that feels good when one is feeling bad, the bad feeling will go away (addiction). Children have been taught to be ashamed of themselves when they cry, and they have been taught that "something bad" will happen to them if they get angry. This training leads to a fear of anger and tears that follows us into adulthood. The process of primal therapy is the process of allowing oneself to unlearn this fear and shame about expressing feelings. The accomplishment of this leads to the unself-conscious expression of anger and sadness. This, in turn, leads to the rebalancing of the natural response mechanism: the autonomic response.

Primal therapy is experiential. One has to allow oneself to feel the feelings that are coming up, within a loving and supportive environment in order to learn that these natural processes are not inherently fearful or shameful. The child does this naturally and unself-consciously (until trained to do otherwise). If its caretakers had consistently provided this loving and supportive environment each time it was needed to process a traumatic experience, those experiences would have been resolved at the time of their occurrence, rather than remembered for future reference. The pool of painful primal memories would not have formed. The adult would not be seeking facilitation, having already had it early on in life.

ABREACTION VS. PRIMALLING

The American Psychiatric Association defines an abreaction as "an emotional release or discharge after recalling a painful experience that has been repressed because it was consciously intolerable. A therapeutic effect sometimes occurs through partial discharge or desensitization of the painful emotions and increased insight."[11]

Janov changed the accepted meaning of this word in order to clarify what he considered to be a crucial difference between experiencing the effects of the recalled imprint in a non-healing versus a healing way. He arbitrarily redefined abreaction as reliving the imprint in a non-healing, non-integrative way. He then defined a *primal* as the reliving of the imprint in a healing, integrative way.

Years later van der Kolk would speak of abreaction as an unmodified reliving of traumatic experience. I think that both men are viewing the process of abreaction in the same way.

If one accepts abreaction as the unmodified reliving of traumatic experience, and, if neurosis is trauma based and caused by intrusion of the imprint into daily life, then all neurotic behavior can be seen as being abreaction. Within the therapeutic relationship, transference and countertransference are also abreaction.

In fact, neurotic behavior is continuous abreaction. It is so common, in fact, that it is mistaken for normal behavior. It is seen as a part of·someone's personality. For instance: "Dad always flies into a rage when no one pays attention to him. It's just the way he is;" "Mom always gets quiet and moody, when someone tells her that she is wrong;"or "Joey is just being Joey" whenever he hurts people with his sarcastic remarks.

Using this definition, Janov's "primal" can now be redefined as "the modified reliving of traumatic experience."

SOME PARAMETERS FOR THE FACILITATION
OF EMOTIONAL WELLNESS

I have argued that all neurotic behavior is trauma based and, thus, has an imprint component that is not accessible or modifiable by reason, behavioral modification, or psychotropic medication. This means that, unless the imprint is addressed, the individual's neurotic behavior, although modifiable, will be forever driven by the force of that imprint. No matter what one does, the imprint will keep intruding into the present context, resulting in the distortion of a person's behavioral response to present sensory information. The neurotic act-out will continue to occur. The integration of the imprint is the only way to resolve the root cause of the chronic condition of neurosis.

Therefore, imprint integration, primalling, or the modified reliving of traumatic experience is the goal of the naturopathic emotional healing of neurosis. A modified reliving dissolves the roots of neurosis in a way that an unmodified reliving, or abreaction, does not: it alters the imprint. Having said this, one needs to ask: how can relived traumatic experiences be modified? How does one primal?

A review of the information presented in this work results in the formulation of some necessary parameters for successfully deconditioning the imprint:

1. In order to modify a conditioned fear memory, the memory must first be released. This involves the breaking down of the protein chain that holds the memory. Because the memory is sensorimotor in content, the released memory is the sympathetic response itself, along with its emotional content. In other words, the client cannot just talk about the anger, fear, and sadness. Rather, the emotional/sensorimotor component must emerge. Once the protein vehicle is broken down—once the sympathetic response is ignited—the memory then becomes modifiable by subsequent experience.

2. The nervous system automatically dissociates overwhelming and uncontrollable experience. It will likewise dissociate the recollection of such an experience if it is recalled in the same intensity. Therefore, the released fear memory must be kept from escalating to such a degree that it is dissociated once again.

3. If the relived experience can be kept within a "sensory window," then the memory data will present itself to image space and, thus, will be reflected upon by the mind's eye, just as ordinary experience enters image space and is

reflected upon. This results in connection. With connection, the encapsulated fear memory gains access to left frontal brain hemisphere functions such as time-contextualizing. Connection results in the integration of the fear memory into the entire psychic structure. Subsequent reliving of the memory is accompanied by the felt sense that it happened in the past. Connection, thus, destroys the continuity of the conditioned neurotic response.

4. If the above steps are accomplished, the client's reliving experience occurs in a controlled way and within a supportive context, which are two vital things that did not occur during the original experience. If the client and facilitator feel comfortable with one another, the client can feel the feeling and the facilitator can support the experience in a loving, attentive way. The model, therefore, for the ideal facilitative environment should be that of the attachment-ordered mother/child relationship.

5. After connection occurs, the facilitator attends to the client's spoken insights about the experience. The emergence of insights after a session is a good indication that a connected feeling occurred. In recognition of the fact that the relived memory is now modifiable and will continue to be for another six hours, the facilitator loads the end of the session with as much positive reinforcement for the client as is possible. And the client is advised to make the next six hours as constructive and upbeat as possible. The idea is to saturate the modifiable fear memory with as much new positive sensory experience as is possible. As the six-hour window closes and the memory is once again embodied in protein for long-term storage, it will contain elements of positive experiential data that it did not previously possess. The client will have restored a partially deconditioned, as well as a positively altered, fear memory. And, any successive retrieval of the memory will be informed by the logic functions of the brain. Any future reemergence of the imprinted data will now be sensed as having taken place at another place and time. It is not happening now.

6. The "coming to know" that accrues to primalled material is not conceptual in nature. The brain is incapable of making coherent declarative memories during trauma. Therefore, a relived fear memory cannot be declarative in nature. Knowing occurs when implicit data is brought into image space for reflection. The mental imaging of fear memory data is sensorimotor in nature. Bringing this kind of data into image space results in a reflection upon nonvisual sensorimotor data. One comes to know about previously

dissociated fear memory content in much the same way that it is known what position in space one currently occupies, without having to actually look at oneself in that position. That is, there is a reflection upon the nonvisual, sensorimotor image that is created by the flow of data from the body's sensory input to the brain. The brain uses this sensory input (which has heretofore been stored in memory) to assemble a nonvisual mental image of one's original experience, which the mind's eye observes (for the first time) and, thereby, begins to understand. Somehow, this event results in the connection of dissociated fear data with left-hemisphere function and, consequently, with the complete psychic structure. The imprint is no longer an encapsulation.

The cellular knowing that occurs with a primal can make a huge behavioral difference. It gives one some degree of choice in subsequent triggered reactions. And, this degree of choice is broadened and deepened in direct proportion to the depth of the sensory reexperiencing.

OTHER ENVIRONMENTAL CONSIDERATIONS IN NEUROSIS

This book has addressed itself to the process of the endogenous toxification of the nervous system and its relationship to neurosis. The continual repression of normal sympathetic and parasympathetic responses is, in effect, self-toxification.

A naturopathic approach to emotional healing also needs to consider the larger problem of *exogenous* toxification of the nervous system. While this subject is too broad to be explored here, there are two general and fundamental areas of inquiry that I studied: the pollution of our food chain with excitotoxic flavor enhancers, a natural consequence of the movement away from consumption of whole foods to the consumption of processed foods; and the stress inducing effect of chronic dehydration.

One of the cornerstone beliefs in the natural health field is that one should eat only whole foods. Instead, most of what people eat today has been processed: packaged, canned, or frozen. All of these foods must have flavor enhancers added to them so that they will taste good even though they are stored for very long periods of time.

These flavor enhancers are called glutamates. Glutamates are naturally occurring amino acids. And the body uses very low levels of these amino acids in the brain as a neurotransmitter. Glutamate is the most important neurotransmitter in the hypothalamus.

There are several brain structures that are particularly vulnerable to the flow of environmental materials through the brain. These organs are called the circumventricular organs. The most important structure, for our discussion, is the hypothalamus. It is the "controlling center for all neuroendocrine regulation, sleep wake cycles, emotional control, caloric intake regulation, immune system regulation and regulation of the autonomic nervous system. In short, the function of the hypothalamus has a profound effect on our behavior."[12]

These structures are particularly vulnerable to the influence of environmental toxins because they lack a blood-brain barrier. This barrier is a tightly knitted protective membrane that has evolved around most of the rest of the brain, which filters out harmful environmental toxins. The brain lacks a lymphatic drainage system and, thus, must be protected from environmental toxins in a different way.

The reason the hypothalamus lacks this barrier is that it must be able to sense the true environmental condition of the blood from moment to moment in order to initiate compensatory body responses to constantly changing environmental conditions. In order to do this, the cerebral fluid makeup (whose source is blood) must closely resemble that of blood.

As was stated prior to this, the hypothalamus uses glutamate in very low levels as a neurotransmitter.

> Glutamate, as a neurotransmitter, exists in the extra cellular fluid only in very, very small concentrations—no more than 8 to 12uM. When the concentration of this transmitter rises above this level the neurons begin to fire abnormally. At higher concentrations, the cells undergo a specialized process of delayed cell death known as excitotoxicity, that is, they are excited to death.[13]

Blaylock concludes that the "careful regulation of blood levels of glutamate is very important, since high blood concentrations of glutamate would be expected to increase hypothalamic levels as well."[14]

It is his belief that the massive flooding of our food chain with neurotoxic flavor enhancers is playing a critical role in the development of neuropsychiatric disorders, learning disorders in children, episodic violence, and many neurodegenerative conditions, such as multiple sclerosis.

Any process of naturopathic emotional healing would, thus, be augmented by a return to a diet of whole food.

As stated earlier in this book, the trillions of cells that go into the makeup of the individual are afloat in a nutrient-rich sea. In a very real sense, the presence of and quality of the water in that sea determines the quality of our existence.

The human body has a built-in water management program. Whenever the body experiences dehydration, a conservation program is initiated, whereby water is taken from less essential parts of the body and shunted to the more vital organs. This condition of dehydration is extremely stressful to the body. Batmanghelidj thinks that chronic dehydration lies at the base of most human chronic disease.[15]

In stress, the body initiates its "fight or flight" mode. The physical effects of this mode on the body are exactly as if the body was being physically threatened. Again, the body cannot distinguish between physical threat and emotional threat. Once the threat is dispatched, the body can release itself from this mode. In the case of chronic emotional stress and chronic dehydration, the body stays in the "fight or flight" mode. The physical effects of staying in this mode are detrimental to the welfare of the body, since the body is essentially feeding off of itself in its efforts to mobilize for a physical, threatening encounter, which never materializes. In other words, it is chronic stress that is harmful to us not stress, per se.

With severe dehydration, even the brain is not getting its ration of water. When the brain starts to dehydrate, cellular energy generation is diminished, setting the stage for chronic fatigue syndrome.

Additionally, a study of waterborne heavy metals and pesticides, which are extremely neurotoxic, is of extreme importance to any discussion of sound emotional health.

A naturopathic, emotional healing facilitator should, thus, teach about the importance of returning to a whole food diet and the adequate consumption of properly filtered water as a way of supporting the emotional healing process.

Finally, since the emotional healing process is supported by physical structure, which, in turn is dependent upon adequate nutrition and detoxification, a broad scope of natural health modalities can be applied to the support of the primal facilitation process. It is logical to conclude that good emotional health can be supported by all natural health modalities.

Chapter 3
Endnotes

1. A. Solter, *Tears and Tantrums: What to Do When Babies and Children Cry*, 2nd ed. (Goleta, CA: Shining Star Press, 1998).

2. S. Turton, "Sam Turton's Primalworks: Thoughts of the Week," *Alternative Emotional Healing*, August 2002.

3. T. A. Stone, *Cure by Crying* (Des Moines, IA; Cure by Crying, Inc., 1995), 9.

4. A. Miller, *Breaking Down the Wall of Silence*, 3rd rev ed. (New York: Penguin Books, 1997).

5. A. Janov and E. M. Holden, *Primal Man. The New Consciousness* (New York: Thomas Y. Crowell Company, 1975), 21-2.

6. B. A. van der Kolk, "In Terror's Grip: Healing the Ravages of Trauma," *Trauma Information Pages*, June 2002. Available: http://www.trauma-pages.com, 6.

7. A. Janov and E. M. Holden, *Primal Man. The New Consciousness* (New York: Thomas Y. Crowell Company, 1975), 22.

8. Janov, *Primal Man, 23.*

9. A. Solter, *Tears and Tantrums: What to Do When Babies and Children Cry*, 2nd ed. (Goleta, CA: Shining Star Press, 1998).

10. Solter, *Tears and Tantrums*, 33.

11. O. van der Hart and P. Brown, *Abreaction Re-evaluated*, February 2005. Available: http://www.trauma-pages.com/vdhart-92.htm

12. R. L. Blaylock, *Excitotoxins, Neurodegeneration, and Neurodevelopment*, February 2002. Available: http://www.dorway.com/blayenn.html, 7.

13. Ibid., 1.

14. Ibid., 7.

15. F. Batmanghelidj, *Your Body's many Cries for Water,* 2nd ed., (Falls Church, VA: 1997).

4

Conclusion

PRIMAL FACILITATION
IS A
NATUROPATHIC MODALITY

Using the principles of naturopathy as a framework, I have explored primal facilitation as a naturopathic practice:

1. *There is a powerful healing power in nature, which can be witnessed in the observation of its natural processes. The body has considerable power to heal itself, and the role of the naturopath is to facilitate this natural process with the aid of natural, nontoxic modalities.*

Solter reasons that children who have experienced traumatic feelings and were not allowed to process these feelings may bring these feelings up later on in the form of unexplainable anger and crying. According to her, this is the body trying to resolve the original traumatic event. As one gets older and fully internalizes the learned processes whereby feelings are kept at bay, it becomes harder and harder to resolve the traumas because of the thickness of defenses that have to be worked through.

Primal facilitation can be thought of as a strongly intentioned attempt to unlearn these defense mechanisms so that this automatic healing cycle can again spontaneously present itself. This time, there is an understanding "witness" present who is able to comfortably listen to the full expression of the anger and sadness. Someone is present who is able to allow the full extent of the anger and crying to occur. The naturopathic emotional healing facilitator understands that a natural emotional healing process is being observed. This natural process is supported by creating a safe environment in which it can occur and by gently nudging the client away from the many defenses that are habitually used to stop the

65

emergence of the feeling. As the client continually sits in this environment it is discovered that it is okay to let feelings out. The many ways (that were previously hidden) in which the client tries to move away from feeling the feelings are discovered. The facilitator is a midwife, who understands the value of sitting in service of the client's natural healing process. There is also the awareness of Hahnemann's belief that a client's native healing powers are so strong that only a small stimulus is needed to begin the healing process. And once that healing process begins, it is best to let the process continue in its own way.

2. *Treat the cause rather than the effect.*

Naturopaths seek the underlying cause of a disease rather than simply suppressing the symptoms. They avoid suppression of the natural healing wisdom of the body, such as fever and inflammation. Symptoms are viewed as expressions of the body's natural attempt to heal; whereas, the causes can spring from the physical, mental, emotional, and spiritual levels.

This is the area of least understanding between conventional and naturopathic medicine.

The naturopathic emotional healing facilitator knows that, by working with repressed fear memories, the client is being helped to eradicate the cause of the emotional, behavioral, and stress-related problems. The symptoms of this repressed memory are the individual's neurotic act-outs. It is understood that the spontaneous expression of the client's highly charged feelings and the subsequent deep crying are an expression of the nervous system's natural attempt to heal itself from previously unprocessed trauma. Therefore, nothing is done to distract the client from the full expression of this cycle once it begins. The behavioral symptoms are not suppressed. The environment in which conventional therapy operates mitigates against this process in several ways. First of all, it usually takes forty-five minutes for a newer client to get to the point of entry of this healing process. This is usually about the time at which the therapist reminds the client that the session has ended. The healing process is, therefore, always being stopped—just as it is about to begin. Secondly, the therapy usually takes place in an office full of breakable items, which abuts other offices having paper-thin walls. In this setting, if a person starts getting into a feeling and gets too loud or too physically active, both the client and the therapist become self-conscious and begin moving away from the feeling. Again, the healing process is stopped just as it is getting started. This type of environment allows for quietly expressed anger and sobbing, and, to the extent that this happens, some healing occurs. But the natural healing process is obviously terribly restricted. So the client's opportunity to heal from past trauma is terribly restricted. The access of traumatic memories requires achieving the emotional intensity in which the memory was originally formed. Why? Because the autonomic fear reaction *is* the memory.

3. *First, do no harm.*

By employing the safe and effective natural modalities, naturopaths are committed to the principle of causing no harm to the client. The naturopathic emotional healing facilitator's actions are guided by a strong belief in the healing power of nature. There is a strong belief in the "wisdom of the body."

Unless there was severe attachment disorder very early in life, which precipitated severe orbitofrontal pruning (resulting in the inability to regulate emotional processing), the nervous system knows, better than any facilitator, when to release repressed feelings, at what pace this should happen, and to what extent this process can safely occur. Therefore the facilitator will never try to "bust" a client's defenses. There is no forced attempt at getting the client to lower defenses. There is never an attempt to force the client into anger and tears. And there is never an attempt to force the client to stay with the process, if the client feels like ending the session. The client's process will naturally unfold within a safe environment, if this is what the client wants to happen. It has a life of its own.

4. *Treat the whole person.*

The individual is viewed as a whole, composed of a complex interaction of physical, mental, emotional, spiritual, social, and other factors. This multifaceted approach results in a therapeutic approach in which no disease is automatically seen as incurable.

Naturopathic emotional healing is based upon the deeply spiritual belief that life is inherently good. The facilitator has a strong belief in the essential goodness of human beings. It is understood that it was the client's inability to get early needs met that is the cause of the present-day disturbing behavior. Had the early needs been adequately met, the client would naturally know how to give love to a mate, to children, and to others. There would not exist a mindless, chaotic, projecting of conditioned anger and anxiety into the world. There would be an attunement with the natural spiritual feelings that are an integral part of the life experience. There would be no need to develop these universal spiritual feelings into exclusionary religious dogmas, which divide human beings from one another. There would be no excessive "pool" of rising pain. So, there would be no felt need to poison the body with alcohol, drugs, excessive food consumption, and similar pain killers. The body's natural production of painkillers (such as serotonin) would not be outstripped, so there would be no need for artificial supplementation of this chemical. Had the early needs been met, there would be the freedom and energy to develop inborn nature to its fullest extent.

The primal facilitator believes that the structure of the human nervous system, with its memory systems, allows the client the opportunity to resolve the early traumas. He also believes that, because of the operation of the fear memory system, the client's fearful past continues to exist within the adult nervous system and that the "past" can be experienced in the present by reigniting the fear memory system. The primal facilitator also believes that reliving will trigger the natural healing response of anger and crying. The restoration of the anger/crying cycle will integrate the fear memories, thereby terminating the body's fear memory intrusion process. The termination of this process means the termination of the neural detoxification process. The client's excessive mood swings and act outs are thereby decreased.

5. *The naturopath is a teacher.*

Naturopaths are, first and foremost, teachers who educate, empower, and motivate the patient to assume more personal responsibility for health by adopting a healthy attitude, lifestyle, and diet.

A naturopathic facilitator cannot prescribe to his client. This is a medical doctor's function. Rather, the function of educator is thoroughly understood. It is rightly assumed that it is the client's responsibility to heal herself. This process requires knowledge of how the repressive process works, and it requires hard work and intention on the client's part. The facilitator can provide knowledge of the process and can join with the client to co-create a safe environment in which the client's self-healing process can unfold. The facilitator studies the various ways in which environmental toxins may disturb the smooth function of the nervous system. So, the naturopathic facilitator teaches natural diet and lifestyle changes that will support detoxification and the proper functioning of the nervous system.

6. *Prevention is the best cure.*

Naturopaths are preventive health specialists. Prevention of disease is accomplished through education and a lifestyle that supports radiant health.

Once the client processes fearful childhood experiences and integrates these memories into the psychic structure, the mindless reactions to internal pain diminish, and the client is better able to feel the importance of giving love and proper care to children and others. If children receive the love and care that they require, they will grow up in good emotional health. The naturopathic facilitator knows that it can take a long time to heal the damaging effects of an unloving, uncaring upbringing. It is understood, therefore, that prevention of this kind of upbringing is the only cure for neurosis.

SUMMARY

Naturopathic Emotional Healing

1. Very stressful and uncontrollable life experiences have the potential to damage the structure of developing self-awareness.

2. The brain recognizes these events as disruptive and automatically isolates the experiences as it would any other toxic compound.

3. This is accomplished by simultaneously disabling high-order memory-making and integration functions (dissociation) and encapsulating the toxic memory within the fear memory system (the amygdalic/primal memory system).

4. The encapsulated memory contains only the feeling components of the experience: the sensorimotor/emotional reaction.

5. The retrieval of fear memories (and all memories) is triggered by the feeling of present events.

6. The recalled primal memory presents itself as a physically experienced conditioned fear response. That is, it is not experienced as a visual, time-contextualized event.

7. The lack of integration of the conditioned fear response makes it seem like present events are causing the emergence of the fear memory.

8. This disconnection from left-brained time matrix function makes the neurotic act-out possible.

9. Primal therapy is the intentional process of triggering these conditioned responses (primal memories) within the limits of a "sensory window," in portions that are insufficient to reactivate the brain's dissociative function.

10. This enables the higher brain functions (the mind's eye) to process this information (for the first time), just as it would any non-traumatic experience.

11. This process automatically connects the encapsulated memory to left-hemisphere frontal brain functions (for the very first time).

12. This connection is called integration.

13. Subsequent neurotic behavior is automatically weakened in direct proportion to the amount of primal memory integration that occurred.

Traumatic life experiences are never truly felt and processed when they occur. Instead, they become fragmented and encapsulated within the primal memory system. Thereafter, and throughout life, the trapped anger, fear, and sadness in these memories is forever surfacing in mindless ways. And, we are forever reacting to them in mindless ways. There is no conscious awareness in neurosis. To the extent that we are neurotic, there is the unconscious living of life. We cannot act with free will.

The good news is that we are given the opportunity to go back and to heal old pain each and every day. The bad news is that this opportunity is not recognized. Instead, we mindlessly use the numbing tools that we learned long ago. And, professional psychotherapy offers only solutions that address symptoms: behavioral modification programs and psychotropic drugs. Either way, we miss the continuous opportunity to feel and to heal.

What would happen if we were presented with the opportunity to unlearn the repressive training that was handed down? What would happen if we trained ourselves to recognize the emergence of fearful memories, whenever they presented themselves? *What would happen if we began to recognize that each emergent and painful feeling was actually an opportunity to begin to heal that old emotional wound?* What would happen if we realized that the only thing we had to do to restore emotional wellness was to let our real feelings out? This is the opportunity presented by the process of primal-oriented naturopathic emotional healing. I have named this process *fear memory integration*.

This represents a call to return to a natural process that was our birthright. It represents an opportunity to restore the balance of the sympathetic/parasympathetic response to life. To the extent that this is accomplished, we can heal forever from the emotional, behavioral, and stress-related problems that are making our present life and relationships painful.

The message given by Arthur Janov over thirty years ago is that there is nothing esoteric or inherently fearful about the unconscious. It is nothing more than a collection of encapsulated, unintegrated fear memories. He referred to this collection as a "pool of pain." Because this type of memory is not integrated, the unconscious is the harbinger of determinism. Because of our neuroses, we are unable to exercise self-control over many of the emotionally important, everyday responses to life. Jung's shadow projection is merely the projection of fear memories onto present-day experiences.

Janov taught that these fear memories can be released. The "pool of pain" can be drained. And, to the extent that they can be released, the unconscious will cease to exist. *Freedom to act intelligently in the present is directly proportional to the amount of fear memory integration that can be accomplished. Free will and primal pain have an inverse relationship.*

The idea of being born "imperfect" or with "original sin" is a consequence of having been brought up in pain that was unconsciously inflicted upon us by our imperfect caregivers. We are all, each generation, imperfect caregivers.

Human beings have no dark or shadow side. Rather, we react to our historic pain in a perfectly logical way: we manifest and project the resultant fear reaction back into the world. We blindly spend our lives mirroring back upon the world the pain that was once inflicted upon us.

Alice Miller has studied the childhoods of people whom history associates with being "evil." Each one of these people was cruelly beaten, shamed, and humiliated as a child. The cruelty that they inflicted upon others as adults was driven by the fear memories of their childhood.

HEALING AND CURING

When Arthur Janov states that his therapy is the *cure* for neurosis, he is speaking of neurosis as though it were a medical disease and he is ascribing to primal therapy an impossible claim.

It is generally understood that a cure is a successful medical treatment in which all evidence of a disease is eradicated. Using this definition of cure and accepting the truth of his idea that neurosis is caused by the chronic intrusion of imprints that form part of a pool of imprints that accrue to all of our traumatic experiences since the twenty-sixth week of conception, we have to conclude that a cure for neurosis would entail the deconditioning of every one of these imprints. Seen in this way, it is clear that the only possible cure for neurosis would lie in the creation of a nurturing environment for the child, from conception on. And it entails the fashioning of an empathetic society, one which unequivocally supports the expression and release of the traumatic experiences that are bound to occur in our imperfect world, at the time of their occurrence. We are a long, long way from achieving this goal.

It is perfectly obvious to all who participate in the primal process that no one is ever *cured* from their neuroses. But most will agree that they have been healed. That is, their lives have been profoundly changed for the better by this process.

Healing is a holistic process. It can be experienced physically, emotionally, and spiritually. It is experienced as a sense of movement toward inner peace and connectedness. It is interesting that Janov uses the word connection to signify a primal event. To him, fluid connection between all levels of the brain is what good mental health is all about. And, the primal process can help the client move toward this goal.

The evidence presented in this book argues strongly for the reexamination of pre-and perinatal practices. It calls for a reexamination of our casual attitude regarding the decision to have children. It calls for a reexamination of the roles and responsibilities of men and women in our society, when it comes to the decision to bear children. For instance, the evidence coming out of attachment theory research runs counter to the politically correct notion that women should, simultaneously, attempt to have babies and careers, at least during the first year of the child's life. It would appear critically important to the proper emotional development of the child that the mother attend to the infant exclusively during this period. And it would seem equally important that the mother's mate strongly and unselfishly support this pair bonding. This sounds old fashioned to the twenty-first-century ear. But an examination of the evidence is compelling.

There should also be a zero-tolerance attitude in our schools toward both physical and emotional bullying.

The primal facilitation process is a powerful tool with which we can decondition the fear memories that are causing us to react improperly in the present. With proper facilitation, our neurosis can be healed, rather than just covered up.

The emotional healing process has nothing to do with understanding and implementing complex psychological theory. Therefore it is not necessary to restrict this kind of work to highly educated theorists. What is needed is the ability and desire to listen to and support one another in nonjudgmental ways. It requires the ability to stay emotionally present with another human being, while that person is expressing deep and honest feelings. It is unfortunate that these skills are not taught to us. And it is even more tragic to see this lack of basic human skill, even in the world of psychotherapy.

The healing of neurosis requires the presence of loving and caring human beings. However, if we are concerned about effecting a cure for neurosis, that must come from the construction of a loving and caring environment for the child, even before it is born. Because of the existence of pain in the world, there must be much more concern about the protection of children from the consequences of this pain. Nature has evolved a mechanism for doing this, and, unfortunately, society has interfered with this natural process.

The bedrock of good emotional health is the genuine desire to welcome and to love the children that are brought into the world. Every child must be loved and wanted. And every child must be emotionally supported each and every time existential trauma occurs. Within such an environment, nature will automatically maintain sound emotional health.

APPENDIX

The Author's Doctoral Practicum Results

The author used his doctoral practicum to conduct experimental research into Janov's claim that primal therapy precipitates measurable and normalizing physical function in the client. Three men, ages thirty-three, thirty-seven, and forty-one, volunteered to undergo twelve weeks, each, of primal facilitation with the author. Prior to this undertaking, the author participated in his own primal therapy at Arthur Janov's Primal Center in Venice, California, doing three consecutive primal intensives there over a three year period. After doing this, he underwent three hundred hours of supervised facilitator training, which he incorporated into his practicum.

The research included both objective and subjective testing prior to and after each twelve-week facilitation. For the objective testing, the participants were each given two salivary cortisol home-testing kits, which were supplied by the Great Smokies Diagnostic Laboratory, Inc. It is known that salivary hormone analysis is an extremely accurate method of stress testing. These tests required that two samples, each kit, be taken at 8 AM and 12 PM of the same day. In each case, these samples were taken by each of the participants prior to the facilitation and immediately after the twelve-week facilitation. All samples were sent to the company's laboratory for analysis. And reports were sent back to the author.

Cortisol and DHEA (dehydroepiandrosterone) are the body's main hormonal stress-coping mechanisms. Cortisol maintains the body's energy levels and responds to stress by precipitating catabolic action, thereby making additional energy reserves available to handle the stressful situation. This hormone also helps to maintain normal blood pressure levels. DHEA, an anabolic hormone, is known to counterbalance the damaging effects of cortisol. An imbalance of these hormones interferes with the body's ability to handle the daily stresses of life. A proper balance of these two hormones, five to 1 cortisol to DHEA, is associated with the maintenance of an optimal stress response.

Objective test results: Prior to facilitation, each participant's cortisol and DHEA levels were determined to be skewed outside of the normal testing range.

After facilitation, each participant's cortisol and DHEA levels were determined to be within the normal testing range.

A questionnaire was designed to test each participant's subjective evaluation of his twelve-week regimen. This questionnaire was predicated upon the hypothesis that spontaneous excitatory reactions such as anxiety, paranoia, compulsive thoughts, anger, etc. were the leading indicators of fear memory intrusion: the cause of neurosis, according to Janov. The questionnaire was given to each participant prior to and after the twelve week facilitation.

Subjective test results: Each of the three participants reported a decrease in incidents of spontaneous excitatory activity at the end of the twelve-week regimen.

Conclusion: Although the test population was statistically insignificant, the practicum results support psychologist Arthur Janov's hypothesis.

Suggestions: The results present a compelling case for repeating this experiment using a population that is statistically significant.

Sources Consulted

BOOKS

Baker, S. M. (1997). Detoxification and healing: The key to optimal health. Keats: Connecticut.

Cummings, S. & Ullman, D. (1997). Everybody's guide to homeopathic medicines. Putnam: New York.

Damasio, A. (1999). The Feeling of what happens: Body and emotion in the making of consciousness. Harcourt Brace & Company: New York.

Frey, W. (1985). Crying: The mystery of tears. Winston Press: Minnesota.

Henderson, D. P. (1995). Panacea! A new non-medical approach to mental health and emotional control. Scientific Specialists: California.

Janov, A. (2000). The biology of love. Prometheus: New York.

Janov, A. (1996). Why you get sick, how you get well: The healing power of feelings. Dove: California.

Janov, A. (1991). The new primal scream: Primal therapy 20 years on. Enterprise: Delaware.

Janov, A. (1983). Imprints: The lifelong effects of the birth experience. General: Toronto.

Janov, A. (1980). Prisoners of pain: Unlocking the power of the mind to end suffering. Doubleday: New York.

Janov, A. (1973). The feeling child. Simon and Schuster: New York.

Janov, A. (1972). The primal revolution: Toward a real world. Simon and Schuster: New York.

Janov, A. (1971). The anatomy of mental illness: The scientific basis of primal therapy. Longmans: Toronto.

Janov, A. (1970). The primal scream. Primal therapy: The cure for neurosis. Dell: New York.

Janov, A. & Holden, E. M. (1975). Primal man: The new consciousness. Crowell: New York.

LeDoux, J. (2002). Synaptic self: How our brains become who we are. Viking Penguin: New York.

Miller, A. (1993). Breaking down the wall of silence. Penguin Books USA: New York.

Mitchell, S. (1998). Naturopathy: Understanding the healing power of nature. Element: Massachusetts.

Morrison, J. (2001). DSM-IV made easy. The clinician's duide to diagnosis. The Guilford Press: New York/London.

Schore, A. (2003). Affect dysregulation and disorders of the self. W. W. Norton & Company: New York.

Schore, A. (2003). Affect regulation and the repair of the self. W. W. Norton & Company: New York.

Solter, A. (1998). Tears and tantrums: What to do when babies and children cry. Shining Star: California.

Stone, T. (1995). Cure by crying. Cure by Crying: Iowa.

van der Kolk, B. (1996). Traumatic stress: The effects of overwhelming experience on mind, body, and society. The Guilford Press: New York.

Vereshack, P. (1993). The psychotherapy of the deepest self. Life Perspectives: Ontario.

ARTICLES

Adrenal Stress: Measuring and Treating. 1–15. Retrieved March 25, 2004, from http://www.blooddetective. com/Articles/AdrenalStressMeasuringTreating.htm

Approaches to the Treatment of PTSD. 1–25. Retrieved August 12, 2004, from http://www.trauma-pages.com/vanderk.htm

Brain Plasticity [Electronic version]. Retrieved January 22, 2003, from http:// www.abc.net.au/rn/talks/8.30/helthrpt/stories/s10302.htm

Brain Plasticity: What Is It? [Electronic version]. Retrieved January 22, 2003, from http://faculty.washington.edu/chudler/plast.html

Corcoran, K. & Maren, S. Hippocampal Inactivation Disrupts Contextual Retrieval of Fear Memory after Extinction. *The Journal of Neuroscience, March 1, 2001, 21(5): 1720–1726*

Emerson, W. Primal Therapy with Infants [Electronic version]. Retrieved July 14, 2002, from http://webpages.charter.net/jspeyrer/emerson.htm

Excitotoxins, Neurodegeneration, and Neurodevelopment. 1–22. Retrieved February 4, 2002, from http://www.dorway.com/blayenn.html

Fitch, P. & Dryden, T. Recovering Body and Soul from Post-Traumatic Stress Disorder [Electronic version]. Retrieved September 15, 2003, from http:// www.amtamasage.org/journal/soul3.html

LeDoux, J. Overview: Emotion, Memory, and the Brain [Electronic version]. Retrieved July 26, 2002, from http://www.cns.nyu. edu/home/ledoux/overview.htm

Memories of Fear: How the Brain Stores and Retrieves Physiologic States, Feelings, Behaviors and Thoughts from Traumatic Events. 1–31. Retrieved December 5, 2004, from http://www.childtrauma.org/CTAMATERIALS/ Memories.ASP

Mendizza, M. Bonding or Violence [Electronic version]. Retrieved August 18, 2002, from http://touchthefuture.org/services/bonding/main.htm

Nader, K., Schafe, G., & LeDoux, J. Fear Memories Require Protein Synthesis in the Amygdala for Reconsolidation after Retrieval. *Nature 406: 722–726, 2000*

Perry, B. Incubated in Terror: Neurodevelopmental Factors in the 'Cycle of Violence' [Electronic version]. Retrieved July 31, 2002, from http://www.childtrauma.org/incubated.htm

Perry, B., Pollard, R., Blakley, T., Baker, W., & Vigilante, D. Childhood Trauma, the Neurobilogy of Adaptation and Use-Dependent Development of the Brain: How States Become Traits [Electronic version]. Retrieved July 25, 2003, from http://www.trauma-pages.com/perry96.htm

Rhodes, J. The Birth Scene: Historical Perspectives [Electronic version]. Retrieved January 20, 2003, from http://www.birthpsychology.com/birthscene/ppic3.html

Scaer, R. The Neurophysiology of Dissociation and Chronic Disease [Electronic version]. *Applied Psychophysiology and Biofeedback, Vol. 26, No.1, 2001*

Schacter, D. Memory: The Fragile Power [Electronic version]. Retrieved January 14, 2004, from http://lcweb.loc.gov/loc/brain/emotion/Schacter.html

Siegel, D. Toward an Interpersonal Neurobiology of the Developing Mind: Attachment Relationships, "Mindsight," and Neural Integration [Electronic version]. *Infant Mental Health Journal, Vol. 22(1–2): 67–94, 2001*

Stevens, L. Does Mental Illness Exist? [Electronic version]. Retrieved June 29, 2002, from http://www.antipsychiatry.org/exist.htm

Stevens, L. The Case against Psychotherapy [Electronic version]. Retrieved June 29, 2002, from http://www.antipsychiatry.org/psychoth.htm

Szasz, T. Is Mental Illness a Disease? [Electronic version]. *The Freeman, Vol. 49: 38-39, November 1999*

Szasz, T. The Myth of Mental Illness [Electronic version]. *American Psychologist, Vol. 15: 113–118, January 2002*

The Effects of Early Relational Trauma on Right Brain Development, Affect Regulation, and Infant Mental Health. 1–80. Retrieved August 13, 2002, from http://www.trauma-pages.com/schore-2001b.htm

The Lasting Effects of Psychological Trauma on Memory and the Hippocampus. 1–9. Retrieved June 18, 2004, from http://www.lawandpsychiatry.com/html/hippocampus.htm

Turton, S. Alternative Emotional Healing. 1–2. Retrieved August 2, 2002, from http://www.primalworks.com/thoughts/thought011022.html

van der Kolk, B. A Hit at ATTACH Conference (Parts I & II). Retrieved March 23, 2002, from http://www.attachmentcenter.org/articles/article020.htm

van der Kolk, B. Posttraumatic Stress Disorder and Memory [Electronic version]. *Psychiatric Times, Vol. 14(3), 1997*

van der Kolk, B. Score: Memory and the Evolving Psychobiology of Post Traumatic Stress [Electronic version]. Retrieved June 25, 2002, from http://www.trauma-pages.com/vanderk4.htm

van der Kolk, B. & Fisler, R. Dissociation and the Fragmentary Nature of Traumatic Memories: Overview and Exploratory Study [Electronic version]. Retrieved June 25, 2002, from http://www.trauma-pages.com/vanderk2.htm

Van Winkle, E. The Toxic Mind: The Biology of Mental Illness and Violence [Electronic version]. *Medical Hypotheses, Vol. 55(4): 356–368, 2000*

Watters, E. & Ofshe, R. Therapy's Delusions: The Myth of the Unconscious and the Exploitation of Today's Walking Worried (Review) [Electronic version]. Retrieved September 27, 2002, from http://www.antipsychiatry.org/br-thdel.htm

Wylie, M. The Limits of Talk: Bessel van der Kolk Wants to Transform the Treatment of Trauma [Electronic version]. Retrieved January 28, 2004, from http://www.psychotherapynetworker.com/jf04_wylie.htm

Young, A. The Secret After-life of Freud's Traumatic Neurosis 1980–2002 (abstract) [Electronic Version]. Vortrag auf der AG-Sitzung am 19. April 2002

Glossary of Terms

ACT OUT—Any behavior that one is exhibiting in a present situation, which is generated by one's response to the internal reality of a triggered primal memory rather than to one's response to the reality of the present situation. This behavior represents a breakdown in the dynamic balance between a person and his environment.

ALLOPATHIC—Any method of treating illness that is premised upon the belief that symptoms are bad and must be dampened through the use of drugs and behavioral modification.

AMYGDALA—An ancient structure located in the temporal lobe of the brain. It links feelings of fear and anxiety to appropriate stimuli and defensive responses. Certain locations within this structure are thought to be a site of memory storage in fear learning. Until the development of our more sophisticated memory system, this may be our only way of remembering our experiences. It contains sensorimotor, rather than visual, data. *The primal memory system.*

AUTONOMIC NERVOUS SYSTEM—The part of our nervous system that regulates the body's internal environment.

CIRCUMVENTRICULAR ORGANS—There are four hollow, fluid filled chambers within the brain through which cerebral fluid flows. These are called ventricals. A circumventricular organ is a brain structure that is located close to one of these chambers.

CORPUS CALLOSUM—A brain structure of about 200 million axons, which connects the left and right hemispheres of the brain. When connection occurs, information from the right hemisphere is transmitted to the left hemisphere through this structure.

CORTISOL—A hormone secreted by the adrenal glands, which prepares us to handle both physical and emotional stress. Elevated levels of this hormone can disrupt the brain's higher thought processes.

DETOXIFICATION—The biochemical processes by which the body rids itself of potentially harmful substances. Toxification, then, can be defined as the end product of a breakdown in these biochemical processes.

DISPOSITIONAL MEMORY—Nonconscious (implicit) memories that are created through classical or operant conditioning. They cause us to automatically respond to things and they happen outside of our conscious awareness.

ENDOGENOUS/EXOGENOUS—Changes that are caused from within (that are self-regulated) are called endogenous. Exogenous changes are caused from some outside source.

HIPPOCAMPUS—A more evolutionarily evolved structure than the amydgala, located in the temporal lobe of the brain. It plays a critical role in spatial memory. Two additional structures in the same area, the entorhinal cortex and the perirhinal cortex, play important roles in object recognition memory. *The hippocampal memory system.*

LYSOSOME—Tiny sacs within the cell that are filled with digestive enzymes. When dangerous microbes are trapped within these sacs they are destroyed or "eaten" by the enzymes.

MYELIN—A fatty substance that coats nerve cell fibers. This coating enables the nerve cells to communicate in a much more efficient manner. It is not until the hippocampal and corpus callosum structures of the brain become myelinated that these areas of the brain begin to function properly.

NORADRENALINE—An excitatory neurotransmitter. It helps the brain to be more alert. The sympathetic arm of the autonomic nervous system uses it to gear up for emergencies.

ORBITOFRONTAL CORTEX—A section of brain located in the prefrontal lobe of the brain, next to the eye sockets (orbits). Damage to this area often results in the inability to inhibit inappropriate behaviors. Very early parental deprivation has been found to damage this site.

PRIMAL—An event that occurs when the sensorimotor components of a conditioned fear response is successfully examined by the mind's eye. This process connects the data with left hemisphere brain functions such as time sequencing.

PROPRIOCEPTORS—Special sense organs that are located near the junction between tendons and muscle, or deep within skeletal muscle tissue. When stimulated, they provide information about the position and movement of different parts of the body.

SEROTONIN—The brain's primary "feel good" neurotransmitter. It acts within the nervous system to block the transmission of physical and emotional pain signals. Drugs such as Prozac work by increasing the brain's amount of available serotonin.

SPROUTING AND PRUNING—A process of nerve development in the brain. At critical times in our early development, millions of new brain cells sprout (grow). If these nerve cells encounter an impoverished environment, such as that caused by severe parental abuse, the cells are pruned (cut away). It is known that early abuse results in an abnormally small orbitofrontal cortex and corpus callosum.

SENSORIMOTOR—Information that is sensory in nature (non-visual) and that causes muscular movement.

SYNAPTIC SPACE—Our nervous system is not wired continuously, as is the wiring in a house. Rather brain wiring is made up of individual nerve cells over which information must travel. Each cell is separated from the next by tiny spaces called synapses. In order for information to cross this space, chemicals (neurotransmitters) must be issued from one cell, they must cross this space, and they must be absorbed by the next cell.

About the Author

The author is an International Primal Association certified facilitator. He underwent his own intensive primal therapy at Arthur Janov's Primal Center. Prior to receiving his PhD in natural health from Clayton College, he earned a Master of Science degree from Rensselaer Polytechnic Institute. He facilitates fear memory integration: a naturopathic, emotional-wellness therapy that he has modeled upon the principles of primal therapy. His work is informed by the latest research in fear memory formation and eradication and post-traumatic stress disorder. He is a certified T'ai Chi instructor and holds a black belt in Shaolin Kempo karate. He is also a graduate of the Men's Leadership Training Program of Boulder, Colorado. He has been a residential rehabilitation specialist for the City of Pittsfield, Massachusetts' federally funded HUD program for 15 years.

978-0-595-36514-2
0-595-36514-0

Printed in the United States
44736LVS00006B